# The New Urban Immigrant Workforce

# The New Urban Immigrant Workforce

## Innovative Models for Labor Organizing

EDITORS

Sarumathi Jayaraman and Immanuel Ness

*M.E.Sharpe*

Armonk, New York
London, England

**Library of Congress Cataloging-in-Publication Data**

Jayaraman, Sarumathi, 1975–
  The new urban immigrant workforce : innovative models for labor organizing /
Sarumathi Jayaraman and Immanuel Ness.
    p. cm.
  Includes bibliograpical references and index.
  ISBN 0-7656-1533-9 (hardcover : alk. paper)—ISBN 0-7656-1534-7 (pbk : alk. paper)
  1. Labor unions–Organizing—United States.  2. Alien labor—United States.
3. Immigrants—United States—Social conditions.  I. Ness, Immanuel.  II. Title.

HD6490.O72U647 2005
331.89′12′0869120973—dc22                                              2004030288

Printed in the United States of America

The paper used in this publication meets the minimum requirements of
American National Standard for Information Sciences
Permanence of Paper for Printed Library Materials,
ANSI Z 39.48-1984.

∞

| BM (c) | 10 | 9 | 8 | 7 | 6 | 5 | 4 | 3 | 2 | 1 |
| BM (p) | 10 | 9 | 8 | 7 | 6 | 5 | 4 | 3 | 2 | 1 |

# Contents

# Acknowledgments

The editors dedicate this work to the memory of Raymundo Juarez-Cruz and Floriberto Hernandez. Raymundo was crushed to death in a supermarket cardboard-box compactor on July 27, 2000, at the tender age of 16 working the midnight shift, and Floriberto, a leader in the struggle for restaurant worker justice, passed away in 2004. Raymundo and Floriberto represent all migrant worker's laboring for dignity and respect on the job.

Saru Jayaraman: I would like to thank my mother and father and sisters, Niru and Madhu, for their never-ending love and support. I would also like to thank Fekkak Mamdouh, my best friend and greatest comrade in the struggle. Many thanks to all of the family at ROC-NY: Rosa Fana, my second mom, Sekou Siby, Stefan Mailvaganam, David Jimenez, Rajani Adhikary, Rekha Eanni, Celine Liu, Grace Gilbert, Magdi Labib, Rafael Duran, Oscar Galindo, and the ROC-NY Board, and our ally Bruce Herman. Also many thanks to my other family at the Workplace Project: Nadia Marin-Molina, Carlos Canales, Zoila Rodriguez, Juan Calderon, and of course Sandra and Maria Claribel Perez, Eduardo Platero, and Jose Canales Chicas. Finally, a million thanks to Aleyamma Mathew, Ebony Bridwell-Mitchell, Hany Khalil, Rinku Sen, and Sameer Ashar for their love and support.

Manny Ness: I thank my colleagues in the Political Science Department at Brooklyn College of the City University of New York. I also thank all my students at Brooklyn College who have challenged me intellectually and made teaching so enjoyable.

The editors are grateful to the Brooklyn College Graduate Center for Worker Education in Manhattan for providing an environment conducive to research and learning on labor and social transformation. We would also like to thank Lynn Taylor, our editor who recognized the importance of this project, and Ana Erlić, who assisted us in getting this book to press.

# The New Urban Immigrant Workforce

# Introduction

Immigrant workers have always received the scraps from the table of the American labor force. Throughout American history, immigrant workers have worked low-skilled jobs for long hours, in poor, often sweatshop conditions, receiving the lowest wages. In the last two decades, however, more than ever, this marginal population has become a substantial, visible force in the domestic economy. With the onslaught of globalization—the unhindered spread of American capitalism by multinational corporations exploiting cheap labor and little regulation in developing nations—the ever-increasing switch to service industries, the dramatic rise in contingent work, and the unceasing growth of the wage gap connected to the erosion of the middle class, immigrant labor and the conditions typical to it have become the norm rather than the exception.

Today's immigrants generally come from areas hardest hit by globalization: Latin America, Eastern Europe, Africa, and Asia. Push-factors include the lack of employment opportunities, devastation of natural resources, and poor remuneration offered in countries of origin; and pull-factors include the promise of employment, even under poor conditions, and the opportunity to send remittances home to family. Once arrived, the immigrant worker of today often gets caught in a cycle of debt and consumption, an exaggerated version of the paycheck-to-paycheck subsistence of most American families. As opposed to prior generations of immigrants, who migrated and left their families behind, today's immigrant workers find themselves in an increasingly globalized world, in which communication with family at home and the ease of travel between destination and origin countries makes the sending of remittances home almost a requisite to the family's willingness to aid in the passage. Alex Julca describes how Peruvian immigrants are often torn between the need to send remittances home, often the major purpose of the journey, and consumption needs that might lead to better employment opportunitie's. With remittances to pay, immigrant workers often end up maintaining the same dead-end positions and conditions year after year, with no hope of advancement. Remittances also foster dependence at home, disruption of families, and inequality in the country of origin. Thus, while some argue that immigrants of today are no more disadvantaged than the Italian or Irish immigrants of the early twentieth century, and will thus be able to assimilate and advance as those groups have done, the combination of industry shift, change in racial composition of newer immigrants, and the increasing requirement to send remittances to family members keeps modern immigrant groups from advancing within the American economy while simultaneously deterring development of their country of origin within the global economy.

An increasing trend in the maintenance of class and working conditions has been the creation of niche markets for particular immigrant groups within global centers like New York City. Informal immigrant networks spread the word within a given ethnic group about a particular employment opportunity that provides a conducive environment for undocumented workers afraid of being deported or easily replaced. Thus, immigrant workers from a particular small town in southern Mexico find their way to remote parts of Long Island to wait on the street corners to be picked up for day jobs, and Africans from neighboring countries find themselves at the same grocery store, to be paid far less than the minimum wage as delivery boys. One of the most visible immigrant communities to have found particular niche markets is the South Asian community, which has glutted the newspaper stand, domestic worker, and taxi industries, among others. Diditi Mitra describes how the Punjabi community of India has found its niche in the taxi driver industry. Whereas South Asian migration patterns to the United States after 1965 consisted largely of educated professionals seeking better technology to suit their education or better remuneration to suit their lifestyle, starting in the 1980s South Asian immigrants have included substantial numbers of low-skill, low-wage, often undocumented workers who seek industry niches similar to those of other low-wage immigrant worker groups. Thus, as wages and working conditions for taxi drivers have deteriorated with certain shifts in the industry, fewer native-born workers and more immigrant workers have found the taxi industry conducive to their needs. Mitra writes that all the Punjabi taxi workers she interviewed cited their low educational qualifications and poor English skills as reasons for taking the job. They had all found the taxi industry through fellow Punjabi-Americans who notify one another about the niche. Industry authorities such as the Taxi and Limousine Commission are ecstatic about the niche development, as immigrant workers, scared by fears of deportation and language barriers, can be easily cowed into paying higher licensing fees and submitting to more strict regulation.

## New Models of Worker Organizing

Clearly, the need for organizing immigrant workers—and for finding unique and creative models adapted specifically to their particular needs—has never been more pressing. The unceasing devastation of home economies has led to the ever-constant flow of immigrants; simultaneously, the rise in service and contingent forms of work has made America increasingly dependent on low-wage immigrant labor. These combined forces have pushed immigrant workers to the front of the agenda for policymakers and the media. Traditional forms of union-model organizing simply do not work in a context in which immigrant workers are terrified to speak out for fear of deportation or indefinite detention, with seemingly insurmountable language and cultural barriers, and contingent work arrangements. Furthermore, the growth of informal immigrant networks and enclaves creates situations in which neighborhood or community organizing (where a particular language and culture is the common currency) needs to be coupled with workplace organizing in order to effectively gain workplace power—including higher wages and better working conditions—for immigrant workers.

To this end, unions seeking to reach out to immigrant workers have had to partner with community-based organizations in order to launch and win successful campaigns in nontraditional workplaces. Immanuel Ness describes how New York City's UNITE Local 169 combined with AMAT, the Mexican American Workers Association, creating the successful Greengrocers' campaign to fight for higher wages and better working conditions for the Mexican workers of several Korean-owned greengrocers in Lower Manhattan. Similarly, Ness describes the unique experience of the Laborers International Union of North America (LIUNA), which re-created the asbestos removal workers' union after the industry had shifted increasingly to subcontracted work and the population of workers came to be comprised entirely of undocumented immigrants. The union used a uniquely effective strategy of recruiting, as organizers respected members of immigrant networks, rather than relying solely on the membership. Using activists from these networks, LIUNA drew upon tactics typical of community organizing rather than union organizing—for example, community-based one-on-one meetings and street actions.

Perhaps some of the most cutting-edge models for immigrant worker organizing have come from the emergence of worker centers throughout the New York metropolitan area. Typically based in worker neighborhoods and focused on particular ethnic communities, these worker centers have combined community and worker organizing models to address a wide range of immigrant worker needs and concerns, including, for example, workers' power within their community. Since they are not constrained by the same restrictions that unions face, these worker centers have been able to find creative models for organizing extremely marginal, contingent workers, in their own language and often outside the intimidation of the workplace.

In her piece about the Workplace Project, a Latino immigrant worker organizing center on Long Island, Saru Jayaraman describes the Alliance for Justice, a new law and organizing model used to create industry-based teams of workers that organize around worker concerns, often in situations in which workplace organizing is difficult or impossible. One of the primary goals of the Alliance is leadership development of team members, in order to provide workers with power in their communities, workplaces, and personal lives. In this way the Workplace Project has the potential to achieve community empowerment in ways where traditional union organizing might stop short. Ai-jen Poo and Eric Tang describe an equally effective strategy in their piece on CAAAV's Domestic Workers United, through which Asian and Caribbean domestic workers have been able to come together in Brooklyn and the Bronx to fight for industry standards concerning hours, wages, and working conditions. Isolated in their employers' homes and less protected by federal and state labor laws than other workers, immigrant domestic workers have been largely ignored by traditional labor unions, who often deem them to be "unorganizable." Domestic Workers United has successfully brought together several immigrant communities, despite language and cultural barriers, developing a core leadership of women of color who take on any and all concerns that arise for their peers, even outside the workplace.

Domestic worker organizing presents a unique challenge in other ethnic immigrant communities as well. In her piece on South Asian domestic workers, Monika Batra explains the need for worker center members and organizers, who better understand the communities in which they are working, to be at the forefront of justice work, providing guidance to lawyers who might provide assistance to the effort. The South Asian domestic workers are most often live-in workers, whose work is constant and all-consuming; organizing in such a context is incredibly difficult. The lawyers' favorite tool of litigation, standing alone, is rarely the most effective means to achieving worker empowerment and justice. Batra argues that a new model of lawyering as support for the more central organizing effort must be the preferred methodology of cause lawyers in the immigrant worker context.

These union-community–based organization partnerships and immigrant worker organizing centers deal with a plethora of worker issues and concerns, from unpaid wages to unjust termination to employment discrimination. A unique workers' center arising out of the ashes of the September 11th tragedy, the Restaurant Opportunities Center of New York (ROC-NY), has become the newest sectoral workers' center in New York City. Saru Jayaraman's piece on ROC-NY describes the ways in which a combination of different sectoral strategies can be used to build power for workers in a particular industry.

The common theme of these pieces is clear: Today's immigrant workers are new, unique populations that face dramatically different industry conditions and require innovative organizing models. While the conditions and challenges facing immigrant workers are discouraging, the call for creativity and the diversity of ways in which organizers have responded is exciting. Our hope is that, by describing the conditions facing some immigrant workers and providing a small sample of the innovative strategies employed to confront them, we can spark further investigation and action, or at least further publication of current action around the New York City metropolitan area. The goal of such action, as we see it, is not the assimilation and advancement of older generations of immigrants, but the increased power and control of new immigrant groups over their working conditions, communities, and lives, in whatever manifestation they deem best for them.

## 2

ALEX JULCA

# Socioeconomics and Conflict in Sending Remittances from New York City's Unstable Labor Markets to Peru

## Socioeconomic Structure and Remittances

The literature on immigrant remittances has burgeoned over the past twenty-five years, along with the phenomenon itself, and yet not much analysis has focused on what motivates immigrants in unstable economic conditions to send remittances to people at their countries of origin. Socioeconomic ties between immigrants and their family (kin) and community (kith) at origin play a significant role as much as the living conditions of immigrants at destinations. This chapter argues that remittances are a result of the dynamics between immigrants' socioeconomic structure and labor market conditions. More important, remittance patterns would also change the socioeconomic relations between origins and destinations of kin/kith. Thus, the kind of socioeconomic structure between immigrants and their kin and ethnic group affect remittance flows, whose patterns ultimately transform that structure also.

This argument can be summarized in the following diagram:

socioeconomic structure     remittances     socioeconomic structure
          (1)                    (2)                   (3)

Before continuing to develop the argument of this chapter, a review of the literature on remittances seems appropriate.

## Literature on the Macroeconomics of Remittances

Broadly speaking, the literature on remittances has focused on the analysis of major geographical areas:

- **Europe:** Southerners such as Turkish and Greek immigrants send remittances from Central Europe.
- **South Asia:** Strong domestic/regional migration as well as immigration to "overseas" destinations such as North America and the Middle East (e.g., Filipinos).
- **The Middle East:** Includes internal migrants (e.g., Egyptians) and immigrants in Central European countries such as France and Germany.
- **Africa:** Northerners (e.g., Algerians and Moroccans) emigrate to Europe, and southerners move to South Africa.
- **Mexico, the Caribbean, and Central America:** Emigrants move primarily to the U.S.

In this sense, a substantial part of the literature on remittances emphasizes two aspects: 1. the economic consequences of remittances on the countries of immigrant origin (Lebon 1984; Keely and Saket 1984; Burney 1987; Hawky 1987; Kandil and Metwally 1990; Brown and Connell 1993; Glytsos 1993; Eberstadt 1996) (see Table 2.1); 2. the consequences of remittances for the local economy and distribution of income (Brown and Connell 1993; Stark, Taylor, and Yitzhaki 1986, 1988; Taylor 1992). For both, some consider positive the economic impact of remittances at countries of origin; others emphasize the negative socioeconomic consequences of remittances. Additional works deal with development issues, proposing new policies to enhance the positive consequences of remittances (Athukorala 1993; Macpherson 1992; Quibria 1986).

Among the negative consequences of remittances, Rubenstein (1992) cites the creation of economic dependence at the national level and the financial dependence at the government and business level. Likewise, Stanton Russell (1986) cites inflation as a potential negative consequence of remittances; Taylor (1992) notes the unequal distribution of income at the local level; and Montes (1990) stresses the tendency of remittances to disrupt the family unit.

Inflation can come from excess demand caused by remittances in the real estate market, from the increase of the mass of money circulating in

Table 2.1

**Positive Consequences of Remittances**

| Authors | Main consequences at origins |
|---|---|
| Keely & Saket (1984)<br>Stanton Russell (1992)<br>Kaimowitz (1990)<br>Portes & Guarnizo (1991)<br>Glytsos (1993)<br>Massey *et al.* (1996) | National and industrial economic growth<br>Reduction of national unemployment<br>Development of human capital (children's<br>  education) |
| Massey *et al.* (1996)<br>Kandil & Metwally (1990)<br>Glytsos (1993) | Economic and social multiplier effects, at the local<br>  and national levels |
| Keely & Saket (1984)<br>Rubenstein (1992)<br>Kandil & Metwally (1990) | Increasing proportion of remittances on  total GDP<br>  (GNP), exports/imports, foreign exchange<br>  reserves, money supply, and total immigrants |
| Stahl & Arnold (1986) | Increasing proportion of remittances on foreign aid |
| Burney (1987) | Increasing proportion of remittances on GDP<br>  (GNP) growth<br>Promote positive balance of payments by<br>  increasing a nation's current capital account |
| Stark, Taylor, & Yitzhaki (1986) | More symmetric distribution of income |

the economy, and/or from the importation of goods whose prices cannot be fully controlled. It is also argued that the impact of remittances in the short run "increases substantially" the inequality of household-farm income distribution, even though "a small equalizing long-run effect" may occur through "the accumulation of income-producing assets" such as animal herds (Taylor 1992, 190, 206). Indeed, household-farm inequality might be exacerbated by the indirect effects of remittances on crop income. On the other hand, it is also stressed that disruption of the primary family unit is a consequence of remittances being directed to fund the immigration of children and the spouse, or vice versa (Montes 1990) as well as because remittances tend to improve the livelihood of nuclear family members, while extended family members are deprived of these new opportunities (Keely and Saket 1984).

## Literature on the Socioeconomics of Remittances

Given the initial motivations for migrating and the character of remittances as aid, it seems natural to limit the analysis to strictly economic consequences at immigrants' origins rather than focusing on the kind of socioeconomic relations and labor conditions from which immigrant remittances originate and develop. Indeed, most studies focus exclusively on standard data on "migrant's income, family income, the rate of interest, the rate of inflation, the exchange rate, the rate of unemployment, and the number of migrants" as determinants of remittance flows (Lianos 1997, 72).

Some literature, however, addresses the socioeconomic structure in which remittances are embedded, either as the motivating and determining factor—section (1)-(2) of the diagram—or as part of broader consequences of remittances—section (2)-(3) of the diagram. In this sense, this chapter partly draws on the works of Stanton Russell (1986) on the sociopolitical consequences of Middle Eastern remittances; Montes (1990) on the socioeconomic consequences of Salvadoran remittances; Pertierra (1992) on the sociocultural impact of remittances in Filipino local communities; and De la Cruz (1997) on motivations and gender differentiation among Mexicans for sending remittances.

Stanton Russell (1986) reevaluates the consequences of remittances by including sociodemographic, political, and institutional variables. She uses an empirical analysis of Middle Eastern and South Asian countries to develop a decisional model called the Remittances System, which highlights the "intermediate relationships between determinants and effects of remittances." Her attention to the socioeconomic characteristics of the family unit as well as to the effects of remittances on transforming kinship ties are salient points in this study. Immigrants send more remittances when the "more immediate family circle" is non-migrant, and less when it has outmigrated. Likewise, remittances are higher when home-country household members are unemployed, and less when there are higher levels of employment at home. She also notes the use of remittances to stimulate socioeconomic independence of household members, especially women and young people, who may even finance their own migration with remittances received.

Montes (1990) describes the results of a survey in which, due to immigration and remittances, living conditions and kin relationships of Salvadoran immigrants in the U.S. are transformed. Mixed consequences follow in El Salvador: Remittances improve the living conditions of lower social classes but polarize income distribution in towns and villages and break the family unit and ties among members. In terms of my initial diagram of causal relationships, this study concentrates on explaining (2)-(3), for example, how socioeconomic relationships are transformed by remittances.

A model maximizing a joint utility function for the "prospective migrant and his parents" is at the base of a "migration contract" theorized by Hoddinott (1994). This case study deals with western Kenya emigrants, who send remittances in currency as well as in kind. The level of remittances "is influenced by" a reward-expected relationship between parents and sons: Parents bequeath land to migrant sons, who remit. Parents and sons may be part of a longer term "implicit contract" that involves "investment in education, migration and remittances, and inheritance." Wealthier parents "can offer a greater reward for remittances." However, certain questions remain unanswered, such as, how wealthy would parents be to still be interested in remittances? Moreover, what kind of rewards would daughter senders expect?

Hoddinot's model reasserts the work of Stark and Lucas (1988) on the "interfamilial implicit contract" of Botswana emigrant households. The latter, however, does not assume parents' and sons' full agreement on the migration contract. In fact, Stark and Lucas propose a "bargaining" model for the "distribution of gains between migrant and home." Yet, both Hoddinot and Stark and Lucas are correct to stress the social interdependence of migration and remittance decisions, in contrast with those who see them as being autonomous and individually based. Finally, both articles suggest that a more general model of intergenerational relations might be appropriate for these African cases. These studies intend to explain (1)-(2)-(3), although the arguments presented do not consider fully the dynamics between socioeconomic relations and remittance flows.

A case study by De la Cruz (1997) distinguishes the motivations for sending remittances according to gender differences, empirically supported by ten interviews by people belonging to five Mexican families from Zacatecas, emigrants to California. She proposes a rough life-cycle model for remittances as a function of kin assets and human capital buildup. This chapter is quite useful for the methodological and analytical approaches, although it focuses on only one aspect of (1)-(2), for example, gender differences, while a thorough consideration of the changes in the socioeconomic structure is missing.

Thus, different sociodemographic models of remittances provide useful insights for the purposes of the present study. Where Stark and Lucas raise the important issue of remittances as social insurance, De la Cruz tackles a detailed analysis of the role of family ties in remittance patterns, and Montes addresses the issue of how socioeconomic relationships evolve in the context of remittances. However, their attention to the centrality of the structure of relations affecting remittances between emigrants and their cohorts at the nation of origin is static and simplified, and does not address the whole dynamics among strength of ties, unstable conditions of labor markets, and kin norms as well as the transformation of socioeconomic ties due to remittance dynamics.

Through my own research of Peruvian immigration to New York City, this chapter synthesizes and develops past studies on the socioeconomic dynamics of remittances. More important, it unveils the tremendous conflict between the strong immigrant commitment to send remittances to Peru and the unstable conditions of work and livelihood in New York. As a consequence, not only do socioeconomic relationships affect remittances, but also remittances lead to rearrangements in the socioeconomic structure. Peruvians have been emigrating from Lima in increasing numbers since the late 1960s, and today there are about eighty thousand in New York.[1]

## How the Socioeconomic Structure Affects Remittances

Migration is often a kin/kith enterprise in which family members and/or friends contribute to funding the immigrants, to facilitating contacts for them at their destination, or to filling the gaps that their absence may create at home. As a consequence, one of the key goals and expectations is the immigrant capacity to send back remittances. Indeed, remittances to kin and kith are the most compelling factor that casts doubt on accounts of immigration that attribute individual maximization of benefits as the primary motivation (Borjas 1995).

So if remittances are the "thing to do" for emigrants, how are their frequency, amount, and uses affected by the socioeconomic role each kin member plays? How does the commitment to remit interplay with the limits imposed by wage levels and job insecurity in New York City? Do remittances conflict with the personal interests of emigrants?

This chapter examines these questions by drawing on direct observations of Peruvian emigrants to New York City in the 1990s. In-depth interviews with forty emigrants belonging to eight households, direct involvement with the Peruvian community in Queens and Brooklyn, and the U.S. 1990 census data are the major sources of information for this chapter. The focus of interest is on the immigrant family household for whom remittances are part of the mechanisms for survival and upward mobility, and whose average income in Peru is no higher than $200 a month, with an average of five household members. Regular money remittances from Peruvians in New York City range between $100 and $300 monthly, depending on economic endowment and number of dependents in Lima as well as wage levels attained. The median income of a Peruvian household in New York City is $28,000 per year, which within the Hispanic community is lower only than Argentinean and Colombian incomes (Rodríguez et al. 1995, 20).

Peruvian middle-class sectors (for whom immigration does not imply sending regular remittances)[2] are not considered in this chapter, nor are the few Peruvian transnational financiers who "fly" their money back and forth according to the differential rates of interest between the U.S. and Peru. Money remittances from Peruvians in the U.S. are on the order of $1 billion,[3] about one-sixth of what the Mexican community remits (see Massey et al., summer 1996) and similar to the amount Salvadorans remit (Montes 1990). In general, the regularity of money remittances and the large number of immigrants involved increase the impact of remittances, despite their small scale at the individual level.

Although the quantity and frequency of remittances may vary, it is well known within the immigrant community that immigrants should send remittances. Ethnographic work confirms this belief, as Jesús, who has three children in Peru, sharply synthesized. "Each month, with or without money for other things, one has to send money to Peru. I do for my children's school . . . some months more than others." Likewise Sophía, a garment worker in Brooklyn, says, "I send $150 every two months to the father of my child who is in a rehabilitation hospital in Lima." Interviews indicate that individuals in the Peruvian community who send remittances are not just the ones who have good jobs, but also the wage earners who are struggling to make a living, often working in two jobs, with insecure prospects and low wages (from five to ten dollars an hour). Thus it would seem that the strength or weakness of the relationship between senders and the recipients plays a significant role, at least as important as the security of the income source. This initial evidence suggests a further inquiry into which kind of initial and evolving socioeconomic conditions at origin and destination are present in determining remittance flows.

The analysis of the impact of the socioeconomic structure on remittances will begin with a definition of structure for Peruvian emigrants. The second part will focus on the tensions brought up between the individual emigrants' interests, New York City's unsteady labor market, and emigrants' responsibilities to people in their home countries. Finally, a third section will allude to the social enforcement mechanisms within the Peruvian emigrant group.

## The Socioeconomic Structure of Peruvians

There are different kinds of social ties among family members and thus varying degrees of obligation to send remittances. Three basic circles of relations tie Peruvian emigrants: nuclear family, extended family, and *paisanos*. See Figure 2.1.

*Ties among Siblings:* Siblings are particularly important in the migration because they have been brought up to support each other as well as their parents. Older children have the responsibility to help raise their younger brothers and sisters, and give advice and support even into adulthood. However, for the same reason and due to the density of reciprocal ties, conflicts among siblings could have a disturbing effect on network dynamics, that is, breakage or transformation of the tie.

*Ties between Children and Parents:* The obligation of children to support and help their parents is well practiced from a very young age. Of her five-year-old son, Rosa would say, "Ya está grande mi hijo, ya me ayuda . . . siquiera para hacer mandados" [My son is already grown . . . He helps me . . . even for simple things such as going to the grocery store or the bakery]. Later, as youngsters earn their first wages, they have to give this in full or share part of it with their parents as a symbol of thankfulness and as "the thing to do." In the case of an only child, this behavior is considered even more obligatory by all members of the family.

For teenagers and adults still living with their parents, which is not uncommon, this moral bond takes on a much more demanding flavor, so that it is considered obligatory to provide parents with some kind of support. This extent of the obligation is affected by the conditions of parents, so that, for example, a single mother is supposed to be supported by her son or daughter more than if she had a husband. The eldest son (less so a daughter), especially in emergency situations, carries more moral and material obligations for both parents and younger siblings.

Figure 2.1 **The Three Basic Circles of Relations that Tie Together Peruvian Immigrants**

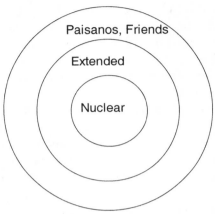

On the other hand, parents might use their skills to help their children, even when they are grown; for example, in the case that parents are construction workers, they might help build or improve their children's homes, either in Lima or New York. María invited her father to New York City on a tourist visa to visit her and his grandchildren, while an additional purpose of this trip was to assist her in the construction of the sewage system for her new house.

*Ties between Husband and Wife:* The relationship between husband and wife is pervaded by accepted norms of conduct. Men are supposed to bring in enough economic resources for the family welfare. For this reason, it is the man's responsibility to look for alternative sources of income in order to support the household; and the wife's income (in case she works outside the home) is not supposed to fund essential household expenditures (for example, food, children's school, clothing). The wife is supposed to administer the resources brought home and allocate them between the children's needs and home improvement. Women, even if they work outside home, are supposed to administer children's personal care, clothing, and other needs.

However, conflicts between this set of norms and the administration of money resources are likely when both husband and wife are wage earners. The capacity of a woman to generate economic resources and assist in meeting household needs on the one hand, and the man's inadequate wage levels on the other hand, conflict with the traditional roles assigned to husbands and wives. In this regard, remittances from wives transform couples' roles, because this income would actually contribute substantially to the household in Peru. In fact, mother emigrants (with or without their children) might already be leaving troubled marital relations behind. And yet, emigrant women who have children still in Lima also try to keep the nuclear family unit alive by sending remittances or by promoting the emigration of children and spouse, because, as Adelaida said, "Children need their father . . . they need both parents for discipline and advice, even more when they are growing up."

*Ties between Unmarried Couples:* The situation for married couples is different from that of unmarried couples. In the case of marriage, the husband's obligations to *spouse and children* back in Peru are strongest, and remittances to them should be larger and especially stable. For instance, even if the female spouse works in Lima, the male immigrant is morally obligated to send remittances to the children.

However, this is not a rigid rule with unmarried couples, in which case the man considers remittances to his partner and children as being more discretionary. Even when the Peruvian legal system states that married and unmarried women have the same right to child support, the custom practiced is that unmarried women with children do not have the same rights as married women. In general, marriage is a more precious asset for women than for men. Single mothers who emigrate try to send regular remittances for their children at home, who later on will probably join them in New York City.

In general, women emigrants who left relatively stable couple relations in Peru tend to keep a strong commitment to their partners and/or children in Peru, which is demonstrated by their sending of remittances for their support in Lima. Stories of young women who emigrated first and funded the emigration of their sweethearts are more common than parallel men's stories.

*Extended Family:* They may provide the same type of information or financial assistance as a nuclear family but are less obligated to do so. Likewise, the obligation to send remittances to members of the extended family is less demanding, except for emergency situations such as sickness or death. There is a hierarchy of obligations according to age and kin proximity: remittances for uncles and aunts precede those for cousins; remittances or help to cousins precede those for nephews. This break in the obligation to assist all family members contrasts sharply with the more inclusive "Swazi society" (Russell 1984) and internal migrants from Botswana's villages in Africa (Stark and Lucas 1985).

*Paisanos (and friends):* Whereas in Peru the term *paisanos* refers to those related by descent from the same geographic space (often from a town in the Andes), in New York City *paisanos* include all Peruvians, and the term might even be extended to other Latino immigrants. It is not rare that ties with *paisanos* and close friends become stronger or equivalent to ties with extended family members. For instance, ties become strong when coworkers are close friends, and mutual aid at the job place is extended to related family activities, that is, parties, weekend events, godparenthood celebrations, and so on. However, there is no sense of obligation to send remittances on a regular basis to friends or *paisanos* unless there is a loan arrangement. A *paisano* might lend money for funding part of the immigration costs such as airfare, visa, "coyote," and room and board. Very likely, this loan is part of a reciprocal exchange of *favores* (favors) practiced even before the emigration enterprise appeared. Trust in the strength of these ties sustains the lender's hope for the loan's repayment. If *paisanos* in Peru have been providers of contacts for jobs or places to stay in New York, they might receive occasional "gifts" from emigrants on particular days of the year, for example, on a birthday, Christmas, or Peruvian independence day.

In general, a more reciprocal type of relationship in the nuclear family will have as a counterpart a more negotiated relationship among *paisanos*. However, conflict between values of solidarity and those of a more market-type (negotiation, goods and service transactions) often haunt Peruvian emigrants. Conflicts partly occur because values, relations, and money involved are not homogeneously measured. We turn now toward these dynamics of socioeconomic conflicts.

### Tensions and Threats to the Socioeconomic Structure

Despite the fact that emigrants cultivate reciprocity values and consider remittances as "the thing to do," there are tensions provoked by the clash among various ongoing personal and social commitments with the bounded amount of income available and the unsteady conditions of the labor market (for example, "insecure" jobs that offer no employee benefits).

### *Unsteady Conditions of Labor Market*

Increasingly, wage levels and secure jobs have been eroded by the deregulation and deindustrialization of the U.S. economy. Thus we often find that Peruvian immigrants work in unstable manual activities. Jobs in construction, jewelry, housekeeping, street-vending, and other factory occupations provide the immigrant with an income to make a liv-

Table 2.2

**Percentage of Employed Peruvians, Hispanics, and Total NY State by Occupational Group, 1990**

|  | Peruvians* | | Hispanics | | Total population | |
|---|---|---|---|---|---|---|
|  | Total | Female | Total | Female | Total | Female |
| Manag. & Professional | 13.8 | 5.9 | 15.8 | 8.0 | 30.0 | 10.0 |
| Tech., Sales, & Admin. | 23.6 | 13.3 | 29.3 | 17.1 | 33.1 | 20.5 |
| Services | 28.4 | 13.3 | 23.1 | 10.0 | 14.4 | 7.4 |
| Precision Prod. & Craft | 13.1 | 1.1 | 10.1 | 1.3 | 9.4 | 0.8 |
| Operators & Laborers | 20.5 | 6.4 | 20.9 | 6.9 | 12.0 | 3.0 |
| Farming & Fishing | 0.6 | 0.1 | 0.8 | 0.1 | 1.1 | 0.2 |
|  | 100.0 | 40.1 | 100.0 | 43.4 | 100.0 | 41.9 |

*Source:* Based on the U.S. Bureau of the Census, Social and Economic Characteristics, 1993. Employed persons 16 years and over.
*Includes U.S.-born Peruvians. Peruvians number about 5% of all Hispanics.

ing in New York City and satisfy the need for sending remittances. For men, construction work and taxi-driving are among the few better-remunerated manual job activities, although construction work has a high seasonal variation. Women working in domestic service, sweat-shops, and selling activities have lower levels of income than men, so women's remittances to family tend to be an even more significant proportion of their income. This trend has sometimes persuaded Peruvian immigrants in New York to have 1.5 or 2 jobs to comply with their personal and social responsibilities. Table 2.2 broadly illuminates class, gender, and race inequalities in New York City by depicting the kinds of jobs in which Peruvians have found regular employment in comparison with their Hispanic and American counterparts.

In this table, 13.3% of Peruvian immigrant women are employed in the service sector (home care for the elderly, cooking, cleaning, babysitting), much higher than the 10% average for all Hispanic women and nearly double the 7.4% average for the total New York City female population. While in the basic office-work category ("technical, sales, and administrative support"), where the work is a little cleaner and less physically stressful, the proportion of Peruvian women employed is 13.3%, much lower than both the 17.1% for Hispanic women and the 20.5% for total females. Peruvian men[4] are more significantly employed in physically demanding "blue-collar" jobs represented by the categories "precision production, craft, and repair" (skilled manual labor) and "operators, fabricators, and laborers" (heavy physical labor). Interestingly, this characteristic is shared by the entire New York City working population, as is the more general trend of just over 40% of women participating in the city's labor market.

The overwhelming majority of Peruvian immigrants are not unionized, and, as noted above, construction work is heavily seasonal. Interviews indicate that the workload in garment factories also tends to vary with the fashion seasons, and, contrary to stereotypes, both men and women are employed in these establishments. As is also clear from Table 2.2, the occupational group most strongly correlated with job security, "managerial and professional" jobs, is the category in which Peruvians are underrepresented: 13.8% of all Peruvians hold such jobs compared to 15.8% of all Hispanics, less than half the 30% held by the total population. The tendency toward insecure employment is also captured in the unemployment figures for Peruvian immigrants in New York City: 8.7% for Peruvians over sixteen years old, 11.3% for Peruvian women (U.S. Bureau of the Census, Social and Economic Characteristics, 1993, p. 313).

Such an unsteady and hierarchical labor market creates cash constraints for Peruvians. However, while the volatility of the New York City labor market may affect the amounts remitted, it does not prevent the regularity of remittances, since one of the main motivations to stay in the city is to fulfill this commitment. Perico, for instance, unable to find work more than three or four days a week, has earned about $5,000 in his first five months in New York City, enabling him to pay for his room and basic board of $350 monthly, send remittances to his wife and two children of about $200 monthly, and pay some debts incurred in coming to America. "If it were not for *mis deudas* [my debts], I would be saving to legalize my residence in the United States, then visit my family in Peru and eventually bring them here," Perico adds.

**Tensions among Socioeconomic Commitments**

Having to send remittances to Peru and—in the case of undocumented immigrants—the need to attend to legalization issues may delay the potential for immigrants' upward mobility. Critical choices confront immigrants regarding socioeconomic commitments at destinations versus their commitments to send remittances to origins. Recent immigrants often have immigration debts and/or a family to take care of financially in Peru, so they are urged to send remittances. On the other hand, fixed costs at destinations such as room rent (often in a family or *paisanos'* apartment), living expenses, and transportation have to be honored. Delays in paying household bills and taking on extra shifts at work are sometimes the responses so emigrants can keep sending the regular amount of remittances. And yet, sociability, reciprocal favors, and loans among kin or kith would ease these tensions. However, personal commitments to achieve upward mobility such as attending school or learning English would be seriously impaired. Under these conditions, the first thing an immigrant tries to do after getting a paycheck and leaving the job for the day is to run into the cash store and then to the travel and remittances firm to deposit the amount to be remitted. This is often accompanied by a telephone call to let the family back home know of the remittance and to show satisfaction for complying with the duty.

## Tensions over Sending to One Family Member or Another

In cases where responsibilities to parents conflict with an immigrant's responsibilities to spouse and children, the accepted priority is to choose the latter, thus to send remittances to sons, daughters, and spouse. In the case of a male immigrant, his responsibilities to his spouse are greater than those of a female immigrant. Yet children are the first priority in either case, and following the results of my interviews, mothers might seem to have a more regular commitment to sending remittances for their children than fathers do. Constraints in a couple's household income mean that parents might be assisted in secret by a married son or daughter, although in emergency situations such as parents' sickness or death, these events take overt priority relative to any other responsibility with spouse and children.

In addition to the hierarchy of family roles noted above, there is also a hierarchy of reasons for sending remittances. Remittances sent on a regular basis include those destined for maintenance of children, single parents, grandparents who represent parents, and siblings' education. Both undocumented and documented immigrants are compelled to comply with these kinds of remittances. Larger amounts of remittances, although for a limited time, are sent for establishing a store, constructing a house, or funding expenses of new kin immigrants. Well-established immigrants tend to varying degrees to get involved with these kinds of remittances. Finally, there are occasional remittances to help grandparents, already self-supporting brothers, and sisters.

## Tensions between Consumption and Remittances

Another kind of conflict may arise, between the immigrant's desire to buy electronic paraphernalia for personal use and the obligation to send remittances. Similarly, a man has to decide between buying new clothes, having some beers with friends, buying a car, or sending a fixed amount of remittances. Buying a car may even improve his possibility of earning a better income or finding a better job, but monthly obligatory remittances for children or parents will prevent or delay this type of purchase. In general, women less easily enjoy this kind of consumption if they have children to support; although men are supposed to pay for dates with women to dinners, movies, and parties.

## Tensions between Institutional and Personal Remittances

Another tension in sending family remittances appears when immigrants feel concern for their compatriots in Peru. The umbrella Peruvian associations and consulate are often not able to reach most Peruvians to collaborate in beneficent activities in favor of institutions and communities in emergency in Peru. This is because the ordinary Peruvian has limited resources to remit to Peru—which are obligated to be sent to family first. Membership in these organizations often also requires payment of a registration fee and monthly dues. It is therefore only well-established immigrants, for example, those who have a secure job plus pension or a private business, who get involved in organizing Peruvian organizations in New York City—whose periodic role is to send remittances (in kind and money) to beneficent institutions in Peru. Leaders in Peru gain personal and political prestige by channeling contributions from the New York business and Latino communities in general. However, organization of social parties with free entrance, with plenty food and drinks for sale, and oriented to the same goals of supporting compatriots-in-need in Peru has better success in terms of attendance and fund-raising.

## Enforcement of Socioeconomic Mechanisms

Nothing is written that enforces an immigrant to send remittances. Aside from repaying related emigration debts, this behavior is due to the self- and group-imposed obligation to send remittances, based on the immigrant's understanding of the family's socioeconomic needs and institutional growth. Any immigrant is aware of the moral penalties and potential loss of ties when deciding whether or not to comply with remittances. Immigrants have internalized the belief that the accomplishment of family duties has subjective and often material rewards.

Remittances are a basic social responsibility that immigrants assume, in particular because the family network has often collaborated to fund the immigrant's emigration. When a person emigrates, social improvement for the family is only potential. The immediate effect is to cut physical contact, particularly difficult in the case of the nuclear family (spouse and/or children). The immigrant needs to send remittances to Peru as soon as possible as a sign that the immigration process is worth the effort and will improve the family's well-being, for example, in food consumption, school supplies, and clothing.

The opinions of the rest of the members of the community, either kin, neighbors, or conationals, are additional factors enforcing "remittance behavior." The immigrant who complies with this norm of conduct gains prestige in the community (inside the family in particular). Indeed, just the fact that the family member is able to live in New York is considered prestigious, which carries a future obligation (somewhat undetermined) to family and community in general. "Adolph is a bad son because he never gave his parents a penny," Duly, a New York City resident whose parents live in Lima, would say of her brother as part of the punishment for one who does not comply with the social network's moral code.

It is implicit that Adolfo will not receive substantial assistance from the family should he need it, a point he understands clearly also. So he will try to regain his family support by eventually returning to sending remittances. In general, when an insecure job puts an upper limit to the regularity of remittance flows, immigrants know what is pending in their relations with their kin or ethnic group in Peru. A weak tie that might break reciprocal obligations is the potential outcome in these cases. Family ostracism may be punishment for an immigrant who gets involved with another mate, leaving spouse and children on their own in Lima. When immigrant parents do not send remittances to their children, this ostracism from the spouse's family, parents, and children may be applied. If a son does not send remittances to his sick father, he is cursed by his siblings and even the rest of the family, and might be considered dead in a literal way.

## How Remittances Affect the Socioeconomic Structure

Thus far the discussion has concerned the socioeconomic relationships that motivate immigrants to send money remittances and the conflicts involved to comply with them within the unsteadiness of New York City's labor market. But as noted earlier, there is a second part to this dynamic, and that is the transformation of relationships through the processes generated by remittances. This section will begin by analyzing some of the relationships immigrants create in NYC to sustain the remittance endeavor, then go on to analyze the impact of remittances on relationships, and conclude with an overview of some of the transformations in relationships that occur, be they positive or negative.

### Remittances: The Economic Dimension of Ethnic Relations

Peruvians forge new relationships and customs in New York City. Whatever the level of wages earned in Peru, the Peruvian immigrant in New York is not just the wage-earner, but the prestigious remitter of dollars. This means that an Ecuadorean immigrant in New York is not a national enemy for Peruvians anymore, but rather another immigrant searching for similar goals and a potential friend or collaborator for finding jobs and providing valuable information. Emigrants become a source of economic resources for nonmigrant relatives as well as instruments for expected upward mobility.

Longer residence in New York implies a greater moral responsibility to assist relatives in Peru, and this means sending larger amounts of remittances or bringing some relative(s) to NYC. Along these lines, the construction of a house, either for the sender's own use in later life or for parents' current use, grants the emigrant material and social prestige. Moreover, the prestige level for somebody who finances a house is higher than for someone who sends money to improve the family's day-to-day consumption, and such prestige may extend beyond family circles. One concrete result may be the request to act as godparent of a child; the expected answer to such a request is acceptance, and godparenthood involves the commitment to give regular advice, gifts, and occasional fully socioeconomic support—if parents die—to godchildren. In other especial situations, such as overseas education or sickness of godchildren, godparents should provide materially for them.

## The Socioeconomics in New York City to Save for Remittances

The need to send remittances despite insecure income leads to the creation of new social ties between Peruvian and other groups of immigrants and to new saving mechanisms. For example, a sine qua non institution where Peruvians create money resources—for remittances and other special expenses—and relations with other ethnic groups is the junta. This financial mechanism is the Peruvian version of the "rotating credit association," documented by Geertz and Granovetter (in Portes 1995, 137–42; see also Besley 1995). A *junta* is a saving/credit system organized by a group of six to ten immigrants, documented and undocumented. The mutual trust developed among the members of the junta is the key to its long-term success. Group members are often related by kinship, *paisano*, job ties, and language. They often include Colombians, Puerto Ricans, and Ecuadoreans. Each member deposits a certain amount of money weekly, and one member has the right to use the total money gathered. For sending remittances in large quantities ($500–$3,000) either for an entrepreneurial venture in Lima or for funding the emigration of a family member, Peruvians often enter into more than one junta. "In this way one could 'see' the money," Jenny asserts. Just as the savings effort and its direction are institutionally channeled, so is the intention to remit.

### Forms and Uses of Remittances

In a clear difference with the Salvadoran or Mexican case, in which emigration to the U.S. is a mix of urban-urban and rural-urban processes (Massey 1987), Peruvians are basically urban-urban immigrants. There are ways in which the general urban-urban character of the uses of remittances pervades the connection of the city of Lima with New York City. While for Salvadorans or Mexicans, using remittances to buy agricultural land is a valid consideration for the future, for Peruvians the construction of a house is part of their major dreams for using remittances. And yet, money is not the only thing needed in order to achieve such a goal: Men, especially construction workers, tend to buy basic tools or machines such as power saws, electrical drills, and so on to be used in Lima.

Another way to categorize remittances is by the capacity of the goods bought to become or create economic wealth. Just as wealth creates wealth, so do remittances for education, housing, generating businesses, or funding further emigration increase the family's assets and capacity to initiate larger enterprises. Remittances may develop human capital by paying for tuition or improve children's facilities for studying. Although food consumption, medicines, and better clothing do not create economic wealth, they may increase human capital in a broader sense.

Immigrant men might be more interested in constructing a house or business in Lima than in bringing their parents or wives and children to New York, unless entrepreneurial ventures they have started might persuade them of the need to bring in family labor. Some Peruvian men fear that life in NYC could change women's household responsibilities and concerns for their husbands. Women are mostly interested in sending remittances beyond the nuclear family as well as bringing other siblings to NYC. However, the positive results of remittances sent for improvement of household ventures in Peru, including entrepreneurial ones, may dissuade would-be emigrants from coming to NYC. This is particularly true when the jobs awaiting them in New York have an increasingly unsteady future and/or the economic and social conditions in Peru are relatively more promising.

A major use of remittance funds is to finance further emigration. Although single emigrants could hope to fund their parents' emigration, brothers and sisters are most likely to benefit from further emigration with the help of family members in America. It is difficult to know if a brother or sister has more of a commitment to help the rest in Peru. And yet, in the cases observed, women have had the clearer tendency to support the emigration of brothers or sisters. Nevertheless, using the 1965 immigration law favoring family reunification, indistinctly sons or daughters conveniently funded the emigration of parents as a first strategic step for promoting further emigration. On one hand, the law allowed single legal residents to bring their parents, and on the other hand legal resident parents could also bring single children to the U.S.

The costs for emigration could drain a large amount of remittances. Peruvian undocumented entrants to the U.S., whose presence was significant from the early 1980s, tend to rely more on kinship relations to draw resources in both origin and destination places. A family often has to raise about $5,500 to $8,000 dollars for travel and board (including the "coyote" stipend) of an undocumented immigrant. A legal immigrant sponsored by some family member draws remittances on the order of $1,500 to $2,000.

The emigration funding of other kin members brings about three basic consequences:

1. Provision of labor for remittance senders' chores or businesses at destination.
2. Redistribution of tasks among household members at origins, according to the role the emigrant used to play.
3. Potential for more or steady remittances in case of still substantial number of dependents at origins.

However, as Stanton Russell (1986, 685) states, "Chain migration supports the notion that, as dependents join the outmigrants, remittances diminish." Accordingly, remittances from married spouses are higher or tend to grow when spouse and children are in Peru than when spouse and children are brought to destinations.

## Changes in Relationships at Origins and Destinations as a Consequence of Remittances

Thus remittances transform the structure of kin/kith, and with them the socioeconomic ties between emigrants and family back home. Of course, some of these intended transformations are the expected result of emigration, such as the ability of an emigrant's children to become better educated. However, other results of the process were never intended by the emigrant.

*Intended consequences:* The potential that remittances have for transforming families in a positive way is vividly illustrated in Pepe's history in New York City: After four years of living in Brighton Beach, today he is a foreman for a private construction company, and the remittances to his parents and brothers have served to construct a sound house in his hometown of Chepén (a northern district about four hundred miles outside of Lima), to establish a grocery store, and to pay the "coyote" to bring his brother to New York City.

Once remittances generate household employment through a business venture at origins, this changes the economic roles of family members. Pertierra (1992, 53) mentions the case of Filipinos buying tricycles that are used for transporting merchandise to the market or people to town. Buying durables and consumption goods changes the consumption behavior at home. Thus, household comfort could also change member roles inside the household; for instance, washing machines may stimulate male siblings to do their own wash rather than having sisters or mother do it, or if products are sent to the home country instead of cash remittances, the young people who receive products can become small entrepreneurs by renting them out for income.

A transformation that might be considered negative or positive could occur at the local village or town level, where "emulation effects" in migrant and nonmigrant families might change their cultural and consumption patterns (Glytsos 1993). Nuclear family members may try to imitate emigrants' consumption patterns by following their tastes for electronic gadgets. In Lima, friends of migrant families would search for information and any sign of wealth brought by emigrants in order to satiate their imagination and appetite for emigrating and consuming imported goods.

A sister who remits money for the self-enhancement of siblings becomes a sort of "second mother." In fact, she becomes de facto mother if the actual mother is absent or dead. In general, these women acquire a more active role and authority inside their families.

Finally, it should be noted that not all transformations involve a change at origin or destination. Regular remittances could also transform the economic role of the sender. For example, Nancy (thirty-eight), traveling as a Peruvian tourist, combines periodic work in a hotel in Long Island with transporting goods for sale back and forth between Lima and New York, while she keeps an eye on and supports her daughters economically in Lima. They could have stayed in NYC except that her husband (fifty-seven) is too old to work in the exigent NYC labor market.

*Unintended consequences:* Yet, in spite of stories of Peruvian emigrants who reunited with their families in NYC, the immigration process itself challenges the continuation of past relationships. These threats take two basic forms: 1. transformation of ties, and 2. breakage of ties. The first tends to be characteristic of relations between parents, brothers, sisters, extended family members, *paisanos*, and friends. However, in cases of unfulfilled commitments among these members, such as an unpaid loan or no remittances sent, these relationships could also break. The second case is also present when the husband or wife emigrates, separating de facto their necessary day-to-day contact, and suspicion of infidelity begins to haunt the minds of separated couples.

The stronger care for family from women is paradoxically what could threaten the relationship when men are the emigrants. Women claim the presence of the husband at home as well as a present father for her children. Thus, their final decision over whether to get involved with other men is often in relation to: 1) their capacity to sustain the various household responsibilities, and 2) their suspicion that husbands have gotten involved with other women in New York City.

According to my interviews and casual contacts with other Peruvians, remittance senders who left siblings and spouses in Peru have a maximum of two years to begin to regularize their legal status (if they are undocumented) and/or bring along some members of their nuclear family, or they face high risks of breaking their initial ties prior to emigration.

The change in the parent/child relationship also has possibilities for a negative transformation. Emigrant parents are economic security providers, but in absence. As a consequence, children who are raised without one of the parents develop new identities. The father loses authority and paternal representation in the household, even while still enjoying social prestige for being in the U.S. and sending regular remittances for his children's maintenance. In general, women at origins tend to have higher participation in income-earning activities and in household administration (raising children on their own and assuming fully economic decisions), or to become emigrants themselves. The fact that mothers could become more economically active enhances the role of siblings, extended family, and outsiders in raising and educating the kids also.

Regarding the impact of remittances on the sibling relationship, in general, established emigrant siblings (remittance senders) form far-distant independent households, altering long-established kin relationships. Remittances, while connecting two living spaces, also seal this separation. Yet this characteristic might not be so novel for Peruvian people, who from the 1940s through the 1960s also altered village relations by migrating from the Andes to Lima. During these years, some kin members developed a separate integration into Lima's society; and even when they maintained contacts with members of the extended family, life in Lima encouraged them to develop new network branches on the job and in the neighborhood. As a result, migrants' children developed even weaker ties with their extended families.

Remittances may weaken ties to extended family. The relations between people who remit and their nuclear family get stronger relative to the relations with their extended family (see also Shankman 1976). Given the extent of the resources required to fund any family member's emigration, there is a tendency for immigrants to support the nuclear family first. For this reason, long-range networks of nuclear family support might weaken the links with non-nuclear relatives and *paisanos*. Some relatives may never receive the assistance they need to come and settle in New York.

## General Conclusions

The discussion in this article of the interaction between socioeconomic relationships and remittances is based on the dual nature of remittances: 1) as crucial economic means for the livelihood of the immigrant-connected working class (money remittances in particular), and 2) as ways to manifest and keep alive a particular social relation, although in fact involving a different one than that prior to remittances. Along the way, the unstable conditions of NYC's labor market impact remittance flows as well as the lives of immigrant families at origin and destination.

Regardless of whether remittances are basically used for consumption purposes or even to create economic dependence in receiving countries, remittances represent kin/kith's capacity to generate economic resources by taking employment in unsteady labor conditions such as they find in New York City. However, income inequality—at the local and even kin level—may be a pervasive consequence, especially when people with different levels of economic endowment have unequal access to the remittance economy.

Remittances are basically intended to improve the economic status of families and thus to keep kin relationships present or alive. However, the unintended consequences of remittances and long-distance emigration are the creation of a new set of kin members' roles, network threads, and actual changes in the initial relationships. These types of changes challenge the economic and cultural bonds of immigrant transnational households.

By sending remittances, immigrants rewrite their own history. The development of new relations at destination defines their immigrant condition while their past relations have a concrete economic representation: remittances. Past relationships "haunt" immigrants, and remittances are one of the main vehicles through which these relations are overtly acknowledged. Paradoxically, it is through remittances that past relations get transformed. For example: A son or daughter is not just the grateful person who shares part of earned income with parents, as was the case before immigrating. Now this person can change dramatically the short- and long-term perspectives for the family by gaining better access to social and economic capital.

Finally, the need to focus on the behavioral character underlying remittance flows and the unstable labor conditions under which these are gathered and sent should now be clear. Along these lines, this chapter has raised the main issues pervading the socioeconomic relationships between remitters and kin/kith. These issues are related to the structure, density, and limits of the ties that shape remittance flows, which then also transform the initial socioeconomic relationships.

## Notes

1. This figure is based on the following calculations: In 1990 there were 32,000 legal Peruvian residents in New York State (U.S. Bureau of the Census, Social and Economic Characteristics, pp. 44, 307). The rate of growth of the Peruvian population in New York between 1980 and 1990 was 100 percent (Rodríguez et al. 1995), so assuming the same rate for the 1991–2000 period, today legal Peruvians in New York City would border 64,000. Based on my interviews, I estimate that this number should be increased by 25 percent to include undocumented Peruvian immigrants, for a total of 80,000.

2. See a similar case for Salvadorans in Montes (1990).

3. Based on information provided by the Inter-American Development Bank (April 2001), the author's estimation of underreported remittances, and interview with the Peruvian bursar of the Asociación de Organizaciones Peruanas de Estados Unidos y el Canada in New York City. However, some specialists have long complained about the general inaccuracy of official remittances data due basically to the unaccountability of informal channels (Stanton Russell 1986, 1992; Choucri 1986; Keely and Tran 1989; Loomis 1990; Brown and Connell 1993; Eberstadt 1996).

4. The data for male employment can be deduced by subtracting the numbers for females from the total figures.

## 3

Diditi Mitra

# Driving Taxis in New York City: Who Wants to Do It?

Although research on the economic incorporation of immigrants has shown the existence of immigrant clusters in specific occupations (Portes 1995; Repak 1995; Waldinger 1994, 1992, 1986; Sassen 1988), scholars differ on their explanations for immigrant incorporation, which in turn leads to the evolution of niches. The debate has generally surrounded the issues of demand, supply, and immigrant networks. The urban economic restructuring perspective focuses on the creation of a demand for cheaper labor that is met by immigrants. In particular, proponents of this urban economic restructuring perspective focus on macroeconomic changes that eventually lead to the incorporation of immigrants into the labor market (Portes 1995; Sassen 1988). The adherents of this perspective argue that postindustrial economic restructuring has contributed to a growth in the service sector that has created a demand for cheap labor, specifically in low-skilled jobs. Growth in the restaurant business that requires kitchen help, messenger services for businesses in urban areas, and household help for the new urban privileged classes are some examples of such low-skilled jobs (Sassen 1988). This demand for cheap labor in these low-skilled positions is met by immigrants.

In contrast, the replacement-labor perspective proposes that vacancies in workplaces that are created due to compositional changes in the labor supply contribute to the incorporation of immigrants into the labor market (Waldinger 1997, 1992). More specifically, a decline in the supply of white workers is key in the creation of opportunities for nonwhites at all levels of the occupational hierarchy, including professional occupations. But immigrants satisfy the vacancies instead of native minorities because the latter are likely to experience discrimination (Waldinger 1997). Moreover, the advocates of this perspective argue that immigrants do not necessarily satisfy a need for cheap labor because the compositional shifts in the workforce occur irrespective of changes in the structure of employment. Thus, the work is not necessarily "cheapened," and immigrants are not incorporated because they satisfy a demand for cheap labor. Nevertheless, immigrants are incorporated because they fill these vacancies created by a decline in the supply of white labor.

Of course, once immigrants are incorporated into a workplace, whether due to economic restructuring and/or compositional changes in the workforce, coethnic network channels are mobilized, which contributes to the formation of immigrant niches. Hence, the network approach proposes that immigrants share close ties with coethnics, which is an important avenue for job search and acquisition (Repak 1995; Portes 1995; Sassen 1995; Waldinger 1994, 1992; Glenn 1985). Since immigrants share information about employment with coethnics, it enables their incorporation. This information within immigrant communities is complemented with the network hiring strategies of employers, who reduce risks by hiring through a network of existing employees (Bailey and Waldinger 1991). Thus, embeddedness in immigrant networks is an important form of social capital because adherence to the normative standards of a network protects the interests of those who are embedded within its structures (Portes and Sensenbrenner 1993). As a result, immigrant niches are likely to evolve once network channels are mobilized in the job search process.

Whereas the urban economic perspective focuses on the structural changes that create a demand for cheap labor, the replacement labor perspective points to the changes in the supply of labor that create opportunities for immigrants. The networks approach highlights the importance of immigrant networks as an important supplier of coethnics who facilitate their incorporation and the formation of niches.

The objective of this article is to examine the issues of demand, supply, and networks as highlighted by the approaches to explain the specific case of the Punjabi[1] taxi driver niche in the New York City metropolitan area. I argue that demand, supply, and networks are complementary in the context of the Punjabi taxi drivers. More specifically, I argue that the shift from the commission to the leasing system within the taxi industry and changes in the supply of a native workforce as well as the formation of strong ethnic networks among Punjabis enabled their incorporation as taxi drivers in the New York taxi industry. The article is organized in the following way: First, I provide an overview of the effects of the shift from the commission to the leasing system on the conditions of work for the drivers as well as its impact on the composition of the drivers. This is important in order to understand why this industry-level change opened opportunities for immigrants. Second, I discuss the changes in the supply of traditional workers that created vacancies in the taxi industry. Like the issue of demand, I assess the impact of this change in the supply of traditional workers on the overall incorporation of immigrants into the New York taxi industry. Third, I discuss the specific case of the Punjabi taxi drivers. Here, I gauge the impact of the broader changes in demand and supply on the Punjabi niche formation. Fourth, I discuss the role of Punjabi networks in the emergence of their taxi driver niche. I conclude the article by assessing the relative importance of demand, supply, and networks on the formation of this occupational niche.

## Data Collection

The data for this study were obtained in the summer of 2000. Interviews were conducted with forty Punjabi taxi drivers. The sample was snowballed because there are no lists of taxi drivers available that would allow for a nonrandom sample. I controlled for biases inherent in this kind of sampling by snowballing from multiple starting points. In addition, eight owners of fleet garages were interviewed. Fleet garages are places that lease taxis to drivers. I obtained names of garages from trade magazines. The sample of managers/owners included in this study was not selected randomly. However, the general recruitment strategies within the industry are much less likely to vary from one garage to another. Also, taxi garage owners are likely to share common interests and perspectives as owners in the industry. Hence, those who were included for this research were likely to illuminate the key hiring practices, express similar points of view on the history of the taxi industry, and have similar interests as owners. Additionally, I spoke with two members of the New York Taxi Workers Alliance (NYTWA) and one official of the New York Taxi and Limousine Commission. I also examined secondary data. The information obtained from these divergent sources allows for a reasonable assessment of the factors that enabled the formation of the Punjabi taxi driver niche in the New York taxi industry.

## From Commission to Leasing: Conditions of Work and the Composition of the New York Taxi Drivers

### *Conditions of Work*

The New York Taxi and Limousine Commission, which came into existence in 1971, approved the leasing system in 1979 (Schaller 1994; Morris 1985). The shift from the commission to the leasing system contributed to a significant decline in the conditions of work for the drivers. Under the commission system, the drivers received a minimum salary plus commission (Morris 1985). The commission system favored the drivers for several reasons. Most important, the drivers could estimate the amount they wanted to earn per shift and could decide upon the numbers of hours they would have to work to do so. This was possible for two reasons. One, the drivers got a base salary under commission. Two, the drivers did not have to earn a fixed amount for the garages. Approximately 47 percent of the total amount earned by the drivers went to them and the rest to the garage (Vidich 1976). As commission drivers, they also did not have to pay for the gasoline used during their shift. The taxi garages, or the fleet owners, were responsible for the gasoline. Furthermore, the drivers had employee status with the garages, which meant that they were entitled to fringe benefits (Schaller and Gilbert 1994).

In contrast, the leasing system increased the financial burden of the drivers in several ways. The redefinition of drivers as independent contractors eliminated the benefits they enjoyed under the commission system. As lessees, the drivers were no longer entitled to a minimum salary. Instead, the drivers had to pay the garages a lease fee. Also, the drivers' income became a variable.[2] Under leasing, drivers begin each shift with a negative amount. In other words, they have to earn the lease money before they can earn for themselves. Moreover, reports show that the actual income of the drivers has declined. According to Schaller and Gilbert (1994), drivers took home $55 in cash per shift in 1981 under the commission system. Their take-home income was $64 per shift in 1986. In 1993 most drivers took home between $75 and $84 per shift. This increase in income is offset by the elimination of fringe benefits, the longer hours worked under leasing, and the rising cost of living (Schaller and Gilbert 1994).

Data on income obtained from interviews of taxi drivers also shows that driver incomes have not increased much. The average income of the drivers at the time of the interview was roughly $93 per shift for an average of six days per week. The average income for owner-drivers,[3] however, is slightly more than for those who were driving with private partners or for garages. The owner-drivers interviewed earned on average $110 per shift. Both groups worked on average six days per week to earn the incomes reported by them. The per annum income for the nonowners and owners was roughly $26,000 and $34,000 respectively. Since Schaller and Gilbert do not provide income figures for the owners, it is difficult to assess whether the figure obtained through interviews increased or decreased. Nonetheless, at least for the nonowner drivers, the increase is insignificant, especially once rising costs of living are considered. Even if a driver was making $84 per shift in 1993, the $9 increase in 2000 is not much. Furthermore, the solidarity of the drivers has been significantly undermined because, as independent contractors, the drivers are precluded from unionizing. This stipulation has hindered the ability of the drivers to negotiate their terms of work. In addition, the seeming flexibility for the drivers under leasing is doubtful as well. Ideally, the leasing system allows individuals the flexibility[4] to work on a need basis. However, drivers who do not have a "steady schedule" are less likely to get a taxi. This way the owners ensure that their taxis are not sitting idle. Thus, drivers who prefer to work on a daily instead of a weekly basis are at a disadvantage.

Clearly the restructured New York taxi industry is an example of "nonstandard employment" (Kalleberg et al. 2000) that increases "employer" benefits because it lacks "explicit or implicit contracts for permanent employment, so [drivers'] employment, work schedules, and earning vary unpredictably, depending on employer needs" (Kalleberg et al. 2000). Such advantages of nonstandard employment are evident in the restructured New York taxi industry. With no guaranteed minimum income, no fringe benefits, and the responsibility for paying other work-related costs, such as gasoline, there are lower economic returns for drivers under the leasing system.

### Leasing and Its Impact on the Composition of the Taxi Drivers

The shift from the commission to the leasing system was accompanied with a decline in the proportion of native-born drivers and an increase in the proportion of immigrant drivers (Schaller 1994; Morris 1985). According to Anne Morris (1985):

No incentives such as increases for commissioned drivers exist in a leasing arrangement, in which what you make is what you earn. Under these
circumstances, the only means of upward mobility in the taxi business is
to buy a medallion, although at current this is an unlikely option for the
average incoming driver. . . . Any combination of the foregoing factors
could have contributed to the changes reported in the composition of the
work force over the past 5 years (p. 47).

In this excerpt, Morris (1985) points to the change in the conditions of
work that contributed to the change in the composition of a workforce
from native-born to immigrant. In a paper presented by Anne Morris and
Alan Foster (1993), the authors show the decline in the proportion of native-born and an increase in the proportion of immigrant drivers as the
number of leasing arrangements increased. Morris and Foster (1993) reported that the proportion of native-born drivers was 26% of the incoming
taxi drivers in 1984. By 1988 the proportion had declined to 14%, and the
proportion had declined to 7.9% by 1992, at which time all fleets had
converted to the leasing system. Another report published by Bruce Schaller
(1994) shows a similar trend in the composition of the workforce in the
New York taxi industry. According to Schaller's (1994) report, there was a
15% drop in the proportion of native-born taxi drivers in New York City
from 1984 to 1991, that is, from roughly 26% to almost 10%. Although
data on the background of drivers are unavailable since the study conducted by Mr. Schaller, the sharp drop suggests a gradual decline in the
proportion of native-born drivers. For the same period, the proportion of
immigrant drivers increased from 74% in 1984 to 86% in 1988 to 92% in
1992. The proportion of immigrant drivers had risen to roughly 91% per
Bruce Schaller's (1994) reports.

The organizers of the New York Taxi Workers Alliance (NYTWA), an
association that voices concerns for taxi drivers, concurred with the reports published by Morris and Foster as well as Schaller. They agreed
that the proportion of native-born drivers declined as garages replaced
the commission with the leasing system. Aslam Khan and Faisal Qureshi,
two important organizers for the association, maintain that the change
in the conditions of work was a disincentive for the native-born. Although Faisal Qureshi, one of the organizers interviewed, was reluctant
to "draw a direct causal arrow" between the shift to leasing and the
reduction in the proportion of native-born drivers, he did state that the
"move out of commission into leasing made the industry less attractive

to white American drivers." Consequently, the proportion of immigrant drivers in the industry increased.

Additionally, the fleet management included in this research pointed out that native-born drivers comprised a larger proportion of taxi drivers until the 1970s, that is, when commissions were still in effect. According to Robert, the co-owner of Wheels Management Corporation, the native-born drivers were not replaced by other native-born drivers. Instead, the proportion of immigrant drivers increased. Yet another fleet owner, Mike, supported Robert's assessment that approximately 60 to 70 percent of the drivers until the late 1970s and very early 1980s were native-born. The owners based their analysis on the background of applicants as well as on the low proportion of native-born drivers at their garages. According to Stavros, owner of Crystal Garage, native-born drivers are less likely to prefer taxi driving because they have access to better opportunities. Stavros argued that even a job at McDonald's pays more than taxi driving. Besides, the risks involved in taxi driving are much higher, he said. There is always the possibility of being robbed by passengers or being physically hurt. The threat to physical safety has always been there for cabdrivers (Vidich 1976), which certainly lowers the attractiveness of the job. The change to the leasing system added greatly to the already existent negative aspects of taxi driving.

The reports of the studies by the NYTWA organizers and the fleet management are supported by an official of the Taxi and Limousine Commission. He, too, reported that there was a significant proportion of native-born Americans driving taxi in New York until the 1960s. Although the official was unable to provide any documentation that would clearly show the backgrounds of the drivers historically, he emphasized that there was a greater proportion of native-born drivers. In particular, he reported that in the period immediately following World War II, there was an interest among the native-born to drive taxis. Since the cost of the medallion was extremely low compared to current rates, many could afford to buy a medallion and become a small business owner:

> It [the medallion] became a steak for people who came back from the war, World War II career, who didn't necessarily have other professional skills but could drive. It was affordable, it was a small business in the sense of any storefront business, you know, a grocery, a luncheonette. Instead of being stationary, it was simply a storefront on wheels, and it was seen as a small business opportunity. And an investment because it had

moderate increases in value over the years. Certainly nothing like what you see in terms of value in the eighties and nineties because it has skyrocketed tremendously and is worth well over two hundred thousand dollars today. But that's really the way it happened. So yes, there were many second-generation Americans who were in the business and continue to be in the business. There is a percentage today of native-born Americans in the business, but it has largely become an immigrant business.

In this excerpt, taxi driving is characterized as "a job of last resort," a characterization consistent with that of the fleet management, the organizers, and the drivers as well as that of Charles Vidich (1976). Nonetheless, those divergent sources point in one direction: They all state that a majority of the workforce was native-born prior to the 1980s, that is, when commissions were still in effect. Thus, the already low attractiveness of taxi driving, which existed from its inception, was increased with this specific change in the wage structure of the drivers. For a profession that already had the status of "a job of last resort," the change to leasing only added to it. In fact, Charles Vidich (1976) in his study of the New York taxi industry has demonstrated that the taxi industry has been faced with a shortage of drivers in times of economic prosperity. Those such as the native-born, who are likely to have access to a wider set of opportunities, are much more likely to move out of the industry. Consequently, the native-born drivers moved out of the industry in large numbers, only to be replaced with immigrants.

The vulnerability of this immigrant workforce is particularly apparent when one considers their undocumented status. Although official reports of the proportion of undocumented drivers in the New York taxi industry are unavailable, interviews with the drivers as well as organizers of the NYTWA indicate that taxi driving is a job that is available for undocumented immigrants. In fact, organizers of NYTWA reported that a significant proportion of the immigrant drivers in the industry are undocumented. Aslam Khan of the NYTWA described the benefits of having an undocumented workforce in the following words:

> I mean it's in the best interest of the businesses in this country to have undocumented immigrants because [business owners] are able to keep people more scared, they are able to not have to follow all the labor laws, they don't have to provide all the benefits, and they think, "This is a vulnerable person who is not going to make demands against me." You know.

As pointed out by Aslam Khan, an undocumented workforce is beneficial for the taxi industry for two key reasons. First, they are much less likely to challenge the poor conditions at work because they are likely to be afraid of making public demands for fear of deportation. Second, they are less likely to look for jobs that require them to show proof of legal residence. Although the Taxi and Limousine Commission requires presentation of work authorization in order to issue licenses, they do not require drivers to present work authorization for renewal of licenses. All the immigrant drivers interviewed for this study said they were not asked to present work authorization at the time of renewal of their licenses. As Faisal Qureshi, another organizer for the NYTWA, said:

> The TLC in the city clearly knows that a significant number of its drivers are undocumented. It's perfectly within their realm of reason and that's fine. So, anything that you call licensing standards, requirements, and so on is constructed within that framework. Okay. For instance, when a driver first tries for hack, he or she has to show a work permit. After you first show a work permit, you never again have to show a work permit. No, the renewals happen by mail. There's no work permit business, nothing. So, it's very clear. A person comes in legal for a moment. Has work permit. Can show work permit.

An expired work permit thus does not prevent renewal of hack licenses. For the taxi industry, undocumented immigrants are a good source of cheap and malleable labor.

Overall, an increase in the proportion of immigrant drivers in the New York taxi industry occurred as the number of leasing arrangements increased. The deteriorating conditions of work attributable to this specific industry-level change is an important factor that accounts for this change in the composition of drivers.

### Changes in Labor Supply in New York City and Composition of New York Taxi Drivers

#### *What Happened to the Supply?*

An already low interest in taxi driving among the native-born due to the nature of the work and the declining conditions of work coincided with changes in the supply of low-skilled native white workers in New York, which created vacancies (Waldinger 1996). In *Still the Promised City*,

Waldinger (1996) argues that erosion in the native white labor supply for low-skilled jobs is an outcome of the upward mobility experienced by native whites. Increases in the education of whites in New York is indicative of the mobility experienced by this group. Whereas the proportion of whites with less than a high school degree sharply declined, from 59 percent to 7 percent from 1940 to 1990, the proportion of whites with a college degree or more for the same years increased from 11 to 48 percent (Waldinger 1996, 86). The skill level of whites had clearly been enhanced. Thus the proportion of whites available for low-skilled jobs had decreased. The positive change in the mobility of whites intersected with their low fertility and high mortality rates, which further diminished their supply. Hence, the effect of the loss of the white worker base was felt even more greatly. In Waldinger's analysis in *Still the Promised City*, the magnitude of that loss is evident. According to Waldinger, "Native white employment in the low-skilled sector declined by over 85,000" in the 1980s (Waldinger 1996, 91). Waldinger continues to argue that improvement in the New York economy in the 1980s, which led to the creation of jobs that required little schooling, did not generate many native white applicants, either. Overall, the proportion of whites in New York in the post–World War II era has consistently declined. By 1950, about a million whites had exited New York. Since then, Waldinger argues, the number has remained the same during the 1960s and continued to shrink (Waldinger 1996, 44). The proportion of whites in the New York population was 43 percent by 1990 (Waldinger 1996, 53). As aforementioned, most whites moved up the stratification order and moved out of the city and into the suburbs. Government efforts to encourage a "suburban lifestyle" only added to the outmigration, according to Waldinger. The construction of housing and roadways paved the path for adoption of the suburbs for whites. What resulted from the diminished supply of white labor was more than 106,000 vacancies in low-skilled jobs in New York (Waldinger 1996, 91).

The low-skilled jobs vacated by whites were filled by unskilled immigrants to New York who arrived in large numbers to the city in the 1980s because native minorities were precluded from these positions due to either their concentration in public sector jobs or discrimination by employers (Waldinger 1996). Waldinger argues that a sharp increase in the city's immigrant population by roughly fifty thousand between 1940 and 1990 benefited the city (Waldinger 1996, 48). By 1990 immigrants comprised 28 percent of the city's population (Waldinger 1996, 48). In particular, the proportion of immigrants from developing nations increased greatly by 1980. Besides legal immigrants, Waldinger points to an overall increase in the proportion of undocumented immigration by 1980. In fact, he argues that the number of "undocumented residents grew by over 50 percent between 1980 and 1992" (Waldinger 1996, 47). The "new" immigration was comprised of both documented and undocumented immigrants. Waldinger also points to U.S. immigration policies of the time as a facilitator of that process. The use of the family reunification provision of the 1965 Immigration Reform and Control Act (IRCA) was one such facilitator of this immigration. This provision allowed immigrants to rely on established immigrant communities in order to emigrate to the United States. Furthermore, the passage of the 1986 IRCA enabled the immigration of low-skilled workers through the Special Agricultural Worker (SAW) provision as well as its amnesty program. This policy and subsequent ones have also aided undocumented immigration. Irrespective of the structural factors that permitted immigration, it created a pool of workers who arrived at a time when New York had experienced a substantial decline in low-skilled white labor. According to Waldinger (1996), immigrants, unlike native minorities, were ready to accept jobs in the lower end of the occupational hierarchy because they arrived with low expectations. In other words, as newcomers, immigrants expect to get jobs that offer low pay and poor working conditions. Therefore, immigrants provided the replacement labor for the low-skilled jobs in New York in the late 1970s and 1980s.

### Change in Supply and the Taxi Drivers

Although Waldinger does not specifically refer to the taxi industry, a decline in the supply of white labor and the employment trajectories of native minorities can be used to explain the high concentration of immigrants in this industry. Besides the poor conditions of work discussed earlier, the upward mobility attained by whites in general is likely to have contributed to their declining proportion in low-skilled jobs, like taxi driving. As for native minorities, their concentration in public sector jobs suggests that they were unlikely contenders for the vacant spots in the taxi industry. If racism further limited the scope for the native minorities in the taxi industry, the data obtained for this research do not show that. But the data do show that native minorities did not provide the replacement labor in the taxi industry. In addition, the greater proportion of undocumented immigrants is likely to have provided the New York taxi industry with a pool of vulnerable workers to choose from.

As the previous section indicated, it is around this time that we see a tremendous rise in the proportion of immigrant taxi drivers in the New York metropolitan area. An industry that experienced a decline in native workers due to worsening work conditions was likely to have been affected even more when the supply dynamics altered. The influx of immigrants to New York City in the 1970s and 1980s is likely to have benefited the taxi industry. This group of largely low-skilled immigrants, which met with constraints in the U.S. labor market, were likely to accept taxi driving despite its declining conditions.

## The Punjabi Taxi Drivers: A Product of Leasing or Change in Supply?

The 1980s witnessed an increase in the proportion of Indian taxi drivers in the metropolitan area of New York (Schaller 1994; Morris 1985). In 1984, Indians constituted roughly 3% of the taxi drivers in New York City (Schaller 1994; Morris 1985). By 1992 they comprised roughly 10% (Schaller 1994; Morris 1985). There was a 7% increase in the percentage of Indian drivers by the early 1990s. Indians had become the third-largest group of drivers, following those from Pakistan and Bangladesh, in the New York taxi industry by 1992, up from their seventh position in 1984 (Morris 1985). Today, based on reports by Faisal Qureshi of NYTWA, Punjabi taxi drivers constitute at least 15%[5] of the drivers in the New York taxi industry, which is still a considerable proportion of drivers in the industry. Given that non–South Asian drivers constitute 40% of the drivers in the industry, it is very unlikely that any one non–South Asian group constitutes 15% of the industry because the 40% is distributed among numerous non–South Asian immigrant groups. Since there have not been any studies done and the New York Taxi and Limousine Commission does not keep any records, the estimates are based on reports of organizers of NYTWA and averages on the proportion of Punjabi drivers in the garages included in this research.

However, the increasing proportion of Punjabi taxi drivers in the New York taxi industry cannot be directly attributed to the shift from commission to leasing. Nor can it be attributed to a decline in white labor. Although the factors of demand and supply as aforementioned contributed to a decline in the proportion of native-born drivers and a simultaneous increase in the proportion of immigrants in the New York taxi industry, it did not have a direct impact on the emergence of the Punjabi driver niche. In order to understand the specific factors that allowed the Punjabi niche formation, it is important to look at the Indian immigration stream to the United States since the late 1970s.

The changes at the level of industry that created opportunities for immigrants coincided with an increase in the proportion of Indian immigrants who had limited skills, for whom taxi driving was likely to be a welcome opportunity. Scholars (Leonard 1997; Khandelwal 1995; Lessinger 1995) have pointed out that this socioeconomic diversification within the Indian immigration pattern began in the late 1970s and early 1980s, when the proportion of middle-class Indian immigrants began to decline. Leonard (1997), further suggests that the overall level of income of Indian immigrants has dropped, particularly since 1985. According to Leonard (1997), the recent waves of Indian immigrants are much less qualified, "show a much lower percentage in managerial and professional jobs, a much lower median income, and a much higher unemployment rate" (p. 81). In fact, Khandelwal (1995) points out that the new Indian immigrants who are less likely to be professionals have been incorporated as taxi drivers, among other "nonprofessional" employment. The "newer" Indians therefore are likely to find their job options restricted. Consequently, taxi driving is likely to be a valuable avenue of income for this group of Indian immigrants.

The educational background of the Indian taxi drivers interviewed for my research matches the profile of the "newer" Indians discussed. With regard to their educational achievements, roughly 38 percent (n = 15) of the sample had a college degree, but approximately 63 percent (n = 25) of the Indian taxi drivers did not. Although the proportion of those with college degrees is still relatively high, they were much less likely to access educational opportunities that would incorporate them into professional categories for at least two reasons. First, the group lacked fluency in English, which limited their job options after emigration. Second, the college degrees held by this 38 percent (15) of Indian immigrants were in fields of study that required pursuit of further education. The majority of drivers interviewed did not wish to do so. Therefore, they were likely to find their employment opportunities constrained. Overall, this group of Indian immigrants was largely from the rural areas of the Punjab and had lower educational qualifications, including a weak command of the English language. Unlike them, the professional Indian immigrants were likely to be urban, holding higher degrees, and likely to be scientists, engineers, doctors, nurses, and so on (Leonard 1997; Lessinger 1995; Saran and Eames 1980). Therefore, the economic trajectory of the Indian taxi drivers included in this study has been much different than their professional counterparts. Even the drivers state that their low educational qualifications and poor English skills are reasons for choosing taxi driving.

Additionally, the increasing numbers of undocumented Indian immigrants who entered the United States in the 1980s (Leonard 1997) are likely to have viewed taxi driving favorably. Surely the illegal immigrants who began to arrive in the United States in the 1980s were likely to perceive taxi driving as an accessible option for employment. As discussed in the previous section, a large proportion of taxi drivers today are undocumented immigrants. It is an accessible opportunity for undocumented immigrants. Consistent with the findings of previous studies, 65 percent (n = 26) of the Indian drivers in my research reported that they used unlawful strategies to enter the United States. Once the immigrants were able to file applications for legalization under various provisions under immigration legislation, they were able to procure work permits, which they used to get hack licenses and become taxi drivers. Since the undocumented immigrants are more likely to be from lower socioeconomic backgrounds (Leonard 1997), their limited skills are likely to "push" them toward taxi driving upon legalization of their status.

The immigration of Indians from poorer socioeconomic backgrounds is likely to have been enabled by the institution of special immigration policies in the United States. Leonard (1997) maintains that opportunities for legalization under the Special Agricultural Workers (SAW) provisions of the 1986 Immigration Reform and Control Act (IRCA) influenced the above-mentioned diversification of Indian immigrants. Then, it is likely that upon procurement of legalization documents, this group was likely to opt for taxi driving, given constraints experienced due to lower educational qualifications as well as poor English skills. In fact, roughly 27 percent (n = 11) of the taxi drivers interviewed for this study got at least a work authorization by filing for legalization under the farm workers' provision of the 1986 act. They were able to get work authorization once they applied for legalization, which then allowed them to get their hack licenses. This specific change in immigration policies eased immigration of unskilled or low-skilled workers who were likely to favor taxi driving given the constraints on employment experienced in the U.S. labor market.

Furthermore, interviews of the taxi drivers included in this research suggest that these legalization policies are likely to have created an image of the United States as a place where immigration restrictions are flexible. Davinder Singh, a forty-one-year-old taxi driver, emigrated to the United States from Germany at the age of thirty because of this flexibility of U.S. immigration policies. He said:

> It was difficult to stay in Germany due to visa problems. There, once your visa expires, you can't stay there. But in the U.S. you can somehow stay here even though your visa expires. If you don't commit any crime, then no one bothers you, you won't be deported. That's the greatest "benefit" of this country, if you don't violate any laws, you can stay here.

Since Davinder Singh found it difficult to remain in Germany, he emigrated to the United States in 1991 on a tourist visa. Later, Davinder Singh filed for legalization of his status under the farm workers' provision. Yet another example is that of Jagteshwar Singh. Jagteshwar was an undocumented immigrant in France. He emigrated to the United States in 1988 to take advantage of the farm workers' provision in order to get legal status in this country:

> But later I found out that you could get the papers here. So, I came back from there. I worked in a farm. They wrote that I worked there for ninety days and I presented those papers to immigration. After that I worked in various places. I worked at gas stations, in factories, I used to get $650 a week. After that I worked for an Indian. He had a clothing factory. . . . After I quit that, they said, "Why don't you get your license?" I came in '88. I got my license in '89. I've been doing this [taxi driving].

The "papers" that Jagteshwar referred to were the legalization opportunity under the SAW provisions of the 1986 IRCA. It allowed him to legalize his status and become a taxi driver in New York City. Nine others in this sample of Punjabi taxi drivers also became legalized under this provision of the 1986 IRCA. However, the experiences of this group of Indian drivers have limited generalizability. Nonetheless, they point to the possibility that other Indians of similar socioeconomic backgrounds were likely to perceive emigration to the United States as viable due these changes in its immigration policies. Hence, such perceptions may have contributed to the increase in the flow of Indian immigrants from lower socioeconomic backgrounds who opted for taxi driving as a source of livelihood.

Yet another event that coincided with changes in the industry and the stream of Indian immigrants was political turmoil in the Punjab, which contributed to an increase in the flow of Punjabi[6] immigrants with limited skills who entered the United States at the same time, that is, in the early 1980s. An excerpt from the interview with Faisal Qureshi points to the economically disadvantaged position of the Sikh emigrants who fled the Punjab as a result of the turmoil. He said:

> Especially in the Indian- and Pakistani-Punjabi, I think that there's a significant relation to land ownership, changes in land ownership patterns in Punjab, to the creation of a wave of emigrants. . . . And . . . but if you go and ask sardars where do they come from: Doaba. It's that narrow strip between the two rivers. You just draw out a narrow strip between the two rivers. It's the Doaba region. I think I can easily say that less than 10 percent come from outside the Doaba. All of them come from inside the Doaba, which means that something happened to that internal economy of the Doaba, which was the agricultural strip during the seventies. It's also connected to the Khalistan movement. I think they got politically persecuted and so the movement out became easier. The desire to move out became stronger. So, I think these are the kind of broad sociological kinds of reasons that we can think of.

Faisal Qureshi pointed to the economic inequalities in the region that pushed Punjabis out. The loss of land by the rural dwellers, according to Mr. Qureshi, has been an important reason for emigration. Studies have also established similar relationships between the conflict and the rural background of the Sikhs that were affected by it (Singh and Thandi 1999). As a result, a significant proportion of Sikhs emigrated. As Aslam Khan of NYTWA said:

> A lot of Sikhs first came here as they were fleeing from some level of political persecution. Even if a person wasn't a political prisoner, just the level of militarization of the Punjab has created a lot of migration.

In the above excerpt, Aslam Khan pointed to the creation of an unstable environment for many due to the political instability in the Punjab. He argues that even those who were not directly affected by the conflict decided to leave as a result of the unstable environment. It is important to note that here I am not suggesting that all Punjabi immigrants to the United States were fleeing persecution. I am only suggesting that it was a part of the flow of the "new" Indian immigration to the U.S.

Thus a confluence of events, such as changes in the New York taxi industry, changes in the supply of white workers, the socioeconomic diversification of Indian immigrants, and political turmoil in the Punjab that occurred around the same time contributed to the emigration of Sikhs who had limited skills and for whom taxi driving was a valuable opportunity. The incorporation of later Punjabi immigrants into the taxi industry and subsequent niche formation, however, is an outcome of the formation of working-class Punjabi communities that resulted from the "new" Indian immigrations. The following section examines the significance of social networks on the emergence of the Punjabi taxi driver niche.

## Punjabi Social Networks and the Punjabi Taxi Drivers

The "new" Indian immigration enabled the formation of Punjabi social networks that tied Punjabis across national boundaries. In other words, it allowed the formation of Punjabi communities within the United States that had social ties with other Punjabis in the Punjab as well. For the Punjabi taxi drivers included in this research, these social connections have been a crucial form of social capital, which they mobilized, that led them to taxi driving.

For the Punjabi drivers interviewed for this study, taxi driving was an outcome of embeddedness in Punjabi social networks dominated by taxi drivers. About 43 percent (n = 17) of the drivers had relatives who were driving taxis, and about another 38 percent (n = 15) had friends who were drivers in the New York metropolitan area. The remaining drivers in the sample had acquaintances who were taxi drivers. The closeness of bond shared with many coethnic drivers is apparent in an excerpt from Gulshan Singh's interview:

> My brother-in-law used to drive. My brother used to drive. My nephew used to drive. That's why I was "inspired" to do this job.

Indeed, three out of four of Gulshan's brothers drove taxis in New York City. The one that did not drive taxis had just arrived in the United States and who was working at a gas station at the time of the interview. On a few occasions I interviewed drivers who were related to each other. The owner of a deli where the drivers take a rest told me that his son was soon to become a taxi driver. On yet other occasions, friends of taxi drivers or relatives who drive taxis would drop in during the interviews. These instances further illustrate the "density" as well as the "multiplexity" (Portes 1995) of ties that the Punjabi drivers had with coethnics in the same occupation.

Through these ties the Punjabi immigrants were able to overcome the constraints experienced in the labor market, due to their undocumented status and/or limited human capital, and adopt taxi driving as a better opportunity. Sukhshinder Singh, a forty-year-old driver who has been driving for the last five years, had the following to say about the predominance of Indians in the taxi industry:

> Indian drivers are not as educated. Maybe one or two. People drive because they speak limited English. They can say, "Hello, sir, where you want to go?" They say two or four sentences and take them to their destination. That's why it's not that difficult. There's no calculation to be made. The job is only to drive. They drive and speak some English. That's why there are more Indians.

After having worked at gas stations, restaurants, a pharmacy, and in an insurance company, Mr. Singh decided to drive taxis. He had friends who were driving taxis when he arrived in New York City, which motivated him to get his license in advance and eventually choose taxi driving as a way to earn a higher income.

The interviews with the Punjabi taxi drivers indicated that becoming a taxi driver is a planned process. Initially the drivers held jobs at gas stations, restaurants or delis, convenience stores, or construction companies because they were either waiting for their hack licenses to be issued and/or waiting to legalize their status. Gurmeet Singh, a thirty-eight-year-old driver who married a U.S. citizen in order to get his green card, aptly summed up the process:

> It's the same for everyone. . . . Usually people do various other jobs for six months or a year and then they do this [taxi driving]. Most important, people don't have the chauffeur license and then people have a problem with their "papers," with a Social Security number, and after you get that you can do the rest. This is a major problem, after you get that, once you get the Social Security, you get work authorization, and slowly get your chauffeur license, and then gradually get into the taxi job.

The process that Gurmeet Singh described is a planned one that is well known to prospective immigrants, who perceive taxi driving as the goal. For this group of Punjabi taxi drivers, their social ties introduced them to taxi driving—an opportunity that was available to them despite their lower levels of skill. For Daler Singh, for instance, his limited educational qualifications increased the attractiveness of taxi driving. He reported that since he did not have any technical skills, taxi driving was a valuable opportunity. He said:

> People said that I can make more money in a taxi, given my qualifications. I hadn't done computer. I am a regular graduate, just completed college. So what can I do with that? I could make good money from driving taxis.

Some consider taxi driving as the ultimate insurance card. About 8 percent (n = 3) of the Punjabi taxi drivers in the sample got their licenses while they were employed in other jobs. This group got their licenses as a safety measure. Although they got their licenses, they did not start driving immediately. According to Daler Singh:

> Many people make their hack license for security. You may not work, but as long as you have the license you can work. When I used to work at a gas station, I made the hack then.

The "many people" Daler referred to, like the others, got the idea of getting the license from coethnics who were taxi drivers. For this group their coethnics had introduced them to taxi driving as a permanent job because of its independent nature. The job for a taxi driver is always available as long as one has a hack license. Thus there is no fear of job loss. Daler Singh was one such driver who had to move back and forth to be with his family. He said:

> I had to go to India every year. I used to be in India for four or five months during summer when the kids were on vacation from school. So if you do that you can't get flexibility in other jobs like you can in taxi. I can take time off and go to India when I want. . . . I'm not the type who just wants to make money and not pay attention to the kids and they won't know you after a while. So I used to be in India half the year and spend time with the kids. So in taxi it's possible to do that.

Mr. Singh's desire to be with his children, his limited educational qualifications, and the networks in which he was embedded influenced his
decision to opt for taxi driving.

Besides, the social ties of the Punjabi immigrants included in this
study allowed them to find taxi driving opportunities within the Punjabi
community. This was available within the community for about 30 percent (n = 12) of the sample within the community. This group drove as
partners of individual owners of medallions who were coethnics. Coethnic
ties as well as the presence of Punjabi owners became an important
source of employment for those who wished to drive taxis. In fact, two
of the drivers who were driving for individual owners had never driven
for a garage. For these two drivers, they had the scope to drive for coethnics from the very beginning of their careers as taxi drivers.

The Punjabi owner-drivers included in the sample, which was roughly
60 percent (n = 24) of the sample, showed a preference for hiring coethnic
drivers. Many even recruited the second driver from their family members. Of the owner-drivers, 27 percent (n = 7) shared their taxis with
relatives. Once this group of Punjabis was able to secure their position
as owners in the industry, they provided employment opportunities for
coethnics, including family members, friends, or even acquaintances.
The Punjabis were therefore able to absorb the subsequent group of
immigrants into taxi driving.

The ability to drive with coethnics was beneficial to owner-drivers as
well as the nonowner coethnics. For the Punjabi owners, the preference
for coethnic partners is probably twofold. First, the limited interaction
of Punjabis with non-Punjabis, as the social ties of those interviewed for
this study indicated, is likely to have lowered the probability of recruiting non-Punjabis. The Punjabis interviewed for this study reported that
their social interactions occurred with coethnics. Thus the Punjabi owners were more likely to find coethnics as partners for their taxis. Second,
the Punjabi owners had a preference for coethnic partners because they
would be better able to control the risks to their businesses. Coethnic
partners would be more likely to be protective of the vehicle if they
wished to avail themselves of this opportunity. Perhaps it would also
lower the risks of car theft, a fear that influences fleet owners to recruit
through recommendation.

For the partners, driving with coethnic partners as opposed to fleet
garages was valuable for two key reasons. First, drivers reported that the
lease rate from individual owners was much lower than that paid to the

garages. While garages lease taxis for approximately $500 a shift, Punjabi private owners lease taxis for approximately $400 a shift. Second, Punjabi drivers reported that driving for a private owner or being an owner allows them to decide on a convenient place to change their shifts, which saves time. Formation and maintenance of social ties thus was beneficial for this group.

In general, the Punjabi immigrants included in this study are embedded within a strong web of social relations where taxi driving not only has become an avenue to maximize income, but also is an opportunity that can be found within the community. Thus it is not surprising to learn that the social ties with coethnics rather than formal labor market strategies to recruit workers directed these Indian immigrants into the taxi industry. The social ties have rendered advertisements for taxi driver positions almost superfluous. Like Gulshan Singh, others also said that magazines did not really help them think of taxi driving as an option. It is the network ties that introduced taxi driving as an idea to the newcomers. Many even thought it was absurd to ask about the role played by advertisements because, according to them, it is only after one becomes a taxi driver that one usually gets a chance to read those newspapers. They are usually circulated at the airports, cab driver restaurants, or the taxi garages, the drivers reported. Not even one Punjabi taxi driver with whom I spoke was influenced by the magazines, such as *Taxi Talk* or *Taxi* magazine or other related newspapers and magazines. The immigrant networks were the only source of information for 100 percent of this sample of Indian drivers.

Evidently, ties with coethnics broadened the scope of economic opportunities for this specific group of Punjabi immigrants. In fact, their social ties helped them overcome the constraints experienced in the labor market due to their limited English language skills, lower educational achievements, and undocumented status. It has also enabled formation of a working-class Punjabi community that is capital-rich and benefits those who are embedded within its structures.

## Conclusion

In sum, the emergence of the Punjabi driver niche in the New York taxi industry is attributable to a combination of several factors. At one level, the industry-level change from commission to leasing in the late 1970s and early 1980s contributed to the deterioration in the conditions of work for the drivers. The leasing system lowered drivers' income as well, as it turned them into independent contractors who were no longer entitled to benefits like employees. This transformation within the New York taxi industry contributed to a decline in the proportion of native-born drivers. Simultaneously, it led to a significant rise in the proportion of immigrant drivers. Around the same time, New York City in general witnessed a substantial decline in the proportion of unskilled white workers. The upward mobility attained by this group as well as a change in their demographics created vacancies in low-skilled jobs. These vacancies were filled by immigrants, who arrived to the city in large numbers during the same period. Both factors of demand and supply generated opportunities for immigrants in general.

However, the broader changes at the level of demand and supply do not explain the incorporation of Punjabis into the taxi industry. To understand that, we have to look at the changes in the immigration of Indians to the United States and specifically examine the diversification in socioeconomic background of Indian immigrants to include immigrants of lower socioeconomic background and/or undocumented immigrants for whom taxi driving was a good opportunity. Changes in the United States's immigration policies enabled the entry of the "new" Indians. These two factors are critical to consider in order to understand why a specific immigrant group is able to consolidate a niche. The broader changes in the industry, Indian immigrants, and immigration policies in the U.S. coincided with emigration of Sikhs due to political and/or economic hardship. Thus not only did the proportion of working-class Indians increase in the late 1970s, it is likely to have been comprised of rural Sikh immigrants who had limited skills.

The "new" Indian immigration pattern enabled the formation of working-class Punjabi social networks that perceive taxi driving as a good opportunity. Through their social ties, the Punjabi included in this research developed a positive perception of taxi driving—an opportunity that allowed them to overcome obstacles due to their undocumented status and/or limited skills. This is probably an important factor that led some to become individual owner-drivers of taxis. It was an occupation that allowed them a higher income and a kind of flexibility that they perceived as being difficult to attain due to their human capital and/or legal status. This group, then, became employers who absorbed coethnics into the business. Clearly, social capital consolidated within the Punjabi community was a valuable resource for this group of Punjabi immigrants.

Overall, the case study of the Punjabi taxi drivers in New York City illuminates the importance of demand, supply, and networks in order to understand their incorporation into the taxi industry. Since the perspectives on immigrant incorporation discussed here operate on different levels of analysis, they explain only a part of the process. Network theory explains immigrant incorporation at the level of the immigrant community and its access to resources. It emphasizes ties with coethnics who have privileged knowledge of resources. In contrast, the urban restructuring perspective addresses the issue at the level of the workplace itself. In other words, it addresses macroeconomic changes that influence changes within an industry, which then create the necessary conditions for immigrant incorporation. It emphasizes the importance of demand. On the other hand, the replacement labor perspective reflects on the changes in the composition of the workforce that allow immigrants to be hired. This perspective emphasizes changes in the supply of traditional workers and its impact on immigrant niches. Clearly, in the case of the Punjabi taxi driver niche, all three apply.

We see clearly that all three factors acted together and shaped the Punjabi niche. Changes in the structure of the industry, decline in the supply of white labor, as well as coethnic ties enabled the Punjabi niche formation. However, the data suggest that there is a need for a group of workers willing to accept work under poor working conditions. Those who have been able to expand their skill level and/or access better opportunities are less likely to drive taxis. Thus, it is reasonable to argue that immigrants are satisfying a need for cheaper labor in the New York taxi industry. They are willing to accept taxi driving under the worsened conditions of work. And, of course, specific histories of Indian immigrants in the United States as well Punjabi immigrant networks have been instrumental in shaping the positive perception of taxi driving that has sustained this niche for roughly fifteen years now.

### Notes

1. The immigrant taxi drivers in the New York metropolitan area are primarily from the northwest Indian state of Punjab. The term "Punjabis" refers to the natives of this state, to their ethnicity. Reports also show that the Punjabi drivers in the New York metropolitan area are primarily Sikhs. Sikhism is a distinct religion. Thus, the drivers are Punjabi-Sikhs. I will use these terms interchangeably in this article.

2. The shift from a commission system to a leasing system was not the first change in the wage structure of the drivers. The drivers were salaried workers from 1911 to 1921. The commission system was, in fact, a setback for the drivers then. If

the drivers failed to produce a certain set amount for the garages, they were terminated (Vidich 1976). However, the drivers were still entitled to a minimum salary as well as other benefits under the commission system. Leasing, however, drastically altered the conditions of work for the New York taxi drivers.

3. The TLC allows individuals to become owners of taxis. These individual owner-drivers have to drive 210 nine-hour shifts annually. For the rest of the shifts they can recruit a codriver.

4. The structure of the work does allow for other kinds of flexibility, which the drivers reported was one of the reasons for choosing taxi driving for those who felt other opportunities were too limited. The absence of constant supervision, freedom to choose the schedule, and the number of hours to work were valued by the drivers included in this research.

5. It is highly likely that Punjabi taxi drivers comprise more than 15 percent of the drivers in the industry. The average proportion of Indian drivers in all the garages included was roughly 19 percent. Hence, they are clearly more than 15 percent in the industry. A low proportion vis-à-vis other groups in the garages is not a good indicator of their overall declining proportion in the industry. Also, the presence of Indians in all the garages sampled for this study is another indication of their strong presence in the industry. Therefore, even when their overall proportion has declined, they still occupy an important position in the taxi industry. Furthermore, garages are not the only source of employment for the Punjabi drivers. Of the Punjabi taxi drivers interviewed, 88 percent (n = 35) were not driving for garages at the time of the interview. They were either owners of taxis themselves or were recruited by individual owners of taxis.

6. The taxi drivers are Indian immigrants of a specific religious and ethnic background. They are primarily Sikhs from the northwest Indian state of the Punjab. Of the South Asian languages spoken by applicants for taxi drivers, Punjabi emerged as dominant (Schaller 1994). Less than a quarter percent of the applicants spoke other South Asian languages (Schaller 1994). Since language spoken is a good indicator of ethnicity in India, that a good proportion of the applicants spoke Punjabi is an indicator of their predominance in the taxi industry. Furthermore, conversations with the fleet management included in this study clearly indicate the predominance of Punjabis. For instance, David Weilerman, owner of Filbert Leasing Corporation, identified all his Indian taxi drivers by Singh. Singh is a last name for Punjabi-Sikhs, an indication of both religion and ethnicity. In addition, the Punjabi taxi drivers in the sample were primarily Sikhs as well, which reflected the religious and/or ethnic background of Indian taxi drivers in the metropolitan area of New York.

## 4

IMMANUEL NESS

# Community Labor Alliances: Organizing Greengrocery Workers in New York City

Globalization and economic restructuring have forced the labor movement to respond to the changing nature of the workforce. This chapter examines an effort to organize low-wage immigrants employed in New York City's greengrocery industry, analyzing a new organizing paradigm—collaboration among low-wage workers, unions, and community groups (the last an element long excluded from mainstream conceptions of union organizing).

After nearly a half century of dormancy, American unions have taken up the banner of organizing new workers to build a larger and stronger labor movement. To achieve that goal, however, requires organizing efforts appropriate to a workforce very different from the workers organized in the heyday of the U.S. workers' movement some sixty-five years ago. The workforce today is significantly more diverse than it was in the 1930s and 1940s, when white male workers in manufacturing dominated the employment landscape. There is a need, then, for strategies that conform to a changing corporate-led global economy. Like their predecessors, U.S. workers today continue to struggle for fair treatment, decent wages, due process, representation, and greater political and economic power.

## The New Global Economy

Industrial restructuring and the growth of subcontracting to small businesses unorganized by unions have occasioned a rapid expansion in low-wage jobs in the United States over the last two decades. Trade unions experienced in industrial organizing techniques increasingly require strategies for reaching workers in these new sectors. In this new environment, traditional campaigns that depend on older industrial models of organizing are not likely to succeed. Ironically, the growth of the global economy and capital mobility has increased the relevance of city-based community organizing strategies that target smaller, spatially dispersed firms that employ relatively few workers.

Although workers are intimately connected to their communities of employment, there is a huge chasm between their workplaces and their neighborhoods. This disconnect was examined by Ira Katznelson in *City Trenches* (1994), a study of the failure of workers to unite around community concerns in the Washington Heights neighborhood of Manhattan. In the United States, the politics of the workplace is very different from the politics of the community. Though we can view workers as holding a large stake in their communities of work, they have almost no power in advancing their needs on neighborhood issues crucial to the survival of their jobs. What power do workers have when rising real estate values lead to exorbitantly high commercial rents, causing their employers to shut down and move? The relocation of industrial employment to low-wage areas in the United States and abroad has significantly changed the social and economic character of New York and other major cities. Industrial jobs in urban factories are frequently being replaced by retail and domestic service jobs where workers work long hours in bad conditions for low wages and with almost no benefits.

## New Immigrants and the Degradation of Work in New York City

New York City, unlike other industrial centers in the United States, never developed a centralized and integrated system of production dominated by a few large monopolist firms employing hundreds or even thousands of workers at a single site (for example, the auto plants in Detroit, or the steel mills in Pittsburgh). With the exception of a few department stores, even retail establishments have tended to be smaller in New York: Only recently have the megastores so common elsewhere begun to appear there. Vertically integrated businesses engender worker solidarity, unionization, labor militancy, and strike activity. By contrast, the horizontal structure of the New York City economy provides a favorable environment for deregulation and declining industry standards, and weakens the ability of unions to organize workers.

Today new immigrant workers in New York and other major U.S. cities are an integral part of the global economy. There is growing evidence that the superexploitation of these workers exercises a widespread pernicious effect, depressing wage levels generally, undermining workplace safety provisions, and hindering union organizing efforts. Although new immigrants are critical to the economy and to the success of organized labor, most unions have tended to ignore them. Recently, however, there is growing evidence that unions are beginning to take notice (Ness and Unger 2000). With new immigrants being increasingly seen as vital to any upsurge in union membership, unions are now actively looking to organize them. At its October 1999 convention, the AFL-CIO called for an end to the employer-sanctions provisions of the 1986 Immigration and Reform Control Act (IRCA), which have penalized immigrant workers seeking to improve their wages and working conditions. In February 2000 the AFL-CIO announced its support for a general amnesty for undocumented immigrants (Bacon 2000).

Though the new rhetoric is indeed welcome, there are few examples of unions actually initiating broad, industry-wide campaigns to organize these new workers. This failure is due in part to the vulnerable status of undocumented workers and the cultural disconnect between union leaders and workers in new labor markets. Successful labor organizing today requires mobilizing and empowering immigrants who do not reflect the demographics of current union membership. An example of such organizing is the ongoing campaign to organize undocumented Mexican workers employed in small delis and greengroceries in New York City, a project that was achieved through bringing together community activists, union leaders, and workers who had begun to organize themselves.

### Stirrings on the Lower East Side

Recent immigrant workers have become part of the fabric of everyday life for most people in New York City. Over the last decade, nearly a million documented and undocumented new immigrants have entered the local labor market, mostly in low-wage industries. New Yorkers are quite familiar with these new immigrants, who perform many essential daily services for them. Immigrants are employed in construction and building rehabilitation, as cooks, dishwashers, and busboys in restaurants, and as taxi drivers, domestic workers, and delivery people (Sassen

2000). A majority are the victims of exploitative employers who force them to accept nineteenth-century working conditions and wages below the federally mandated minimum of $5.15 an hour. In the greengrocery industry, workers who clean, prepare, and package fruit and vegetables are required to work twelve-hour days, six days a week, with no overtime pay or medical benefits. They receive wages well below the minimum, typically earning $250 for a 72-hour week (less than $3.50 per hour). When workers try to improve these conditions or join unions, they are fired and replaced with other recent immigrants. There are over 2,000 greengroceries in New York City, employing 14,000 workers, mostly Mexicans, who work in conditions similar to workers in garment industry sweatshops. Most of the employers in the industry are Korean immigrants, whose establishments vary greatly in size from small shops employing two or three workers to larger markets employing twenty-five or more. Many own more than one shop.

The current effort to organize immigrant workers began in 1998 with the formation of the Lower East Side Community Labor Coalition (CLC), an alliance of progressive organizations dedicated to defending and improving the conditions of immigrant workers employed in the neighborhood. The coalition initially comprised two main groups: the Coalition for a District Alternative (CODA) and the Lower East Side Collective (LESC). CODA, a multiracial community organization, was formed in 1992 by veteran activists who sought to advance their agenda in the electoral realm while continuing to mobilize neighborhood residents around issues of concern (affordable housing, quality education, the environment, police brutality, and the like). LESC had come together in early 1997 as an organizing focus for younger activists looking to become involved locally. Although it did not take an explicitly electoral tack, many of its members (some of whom also joined CODA) worked that summer and fall to elect CODA cofounder Margarita López to the city council. That insurgent campaign, against an opponent backed solidly by mainstream politicians and labor unions, scored a stunning upset that even today is hailed citywide as a triumph of grassroots organizing. After victory in the September primary (tantamount to election in overwhelmingly Democratic New York City), Ernesto Jofre, the only labor leader to have supported the campaign, let CODA know that he would welcome a collaboration between the Lower East Side Collective and his union, Local 169 of UNITE (Union of Needletrades, Industrial, and Textile Employees) now UNITE-HERE.

Later that fall, CODA and LESC members interested in workers' rights began meeting to discuss how immigrant workers in local businesses could be engaged and community support be built for a campaign to improve wages and working conditions. By January 1998 the CLC was formally in existence and actively involved in a campaign to make the Lower East Side a Living Wage Zone. Restaurants were chosen as the initial focus, as gentrification of the area had brought a proliferation of upscale eateries. They presented the stark contrast of well-heeled diners eating pricey food served up by immigrant kitchen-help making substandard wages. A pamphlet—*What's the Real Cost of Dinner of the Lower East Side?*—was produced to educate consumers, while English as a second language (ESL) classes were set up at Charas/El Bohio, a local community center, and promoted among the workers in an effort to have contact with them away from their employers. Inquiries were made to the Hotel Employees and Restaurant Employees (HERE), now UNITE-HERE. Local 100, to honor their jurisdiction, but they were concentrating on cafeterias and larger restaurants uptown.

Meanwhile, engaging workers in the Lower East Side was proving extremely difficult. Impediments included the implanted wariness of immigrants, the fact that few CLCers were fluent in Spanish, the difficulty of contacting workers for the most part confined to kitchens, and the problem of scheduling ESL classes these workers could attend, given their long and grueling hours. The campaign seemed stalled.

**The Mexican American Workers Association**

Then, in April 1998, the character of the campaign changed dramatically. CLC members happened one afternoon upon a small but lively demonstration in front of Leshko's, an old-style Ukrainian coffee shop on Avenue A. There a group called the Asociación Mexicano—Americano de Trabajadores (AMAT—Mexican-American Workers Association) was protesting the unfair firing of two workers and demanding that they be paid the back wages owed them. Jerry Dominguez, the group's founder and lead organizer, said actions of this sort were used wherever AMAT learned of abuses and was asked to help. Based in El Barrio (East Harlem), the group had built up an extensive network of contacts with Mexican immigrant workers throughout the city, particularly in delis and greengroceries, where workers have more contact with the public and so are more accessible to organizers.

A week later the demonstrators were back, now greatly augmented by CLC activists. Patrons were asked to boycott the restaurant, and most complied; within an hour or two the owner had relented and agreed to a settlement. CLC had found the partner it needed. In short order AMAT agreed to join the coalition, and plans were laid to redirect the campaign toward workers in the neighborhood's twenty or so greengroceries.

The idea was to move beyond the reactive struggles AMAT had been waging in particularly egregious instances of abuse. However successful in righting individual wrongs, these actions did little to change the general pattern of day-in, day-out abuse endemic to the industry. An employer could be forced to cough up wages that were owed, but the industry-wide practice of paying well below the legal minimum went untouched. It was thought that by harnessing worker militancy to a community's power to boycott, a more permanent and general improvement in wages and working conditions could be achieved. A community presence would protect these very vulnerable workers from summary firings or exposure to the Immigration and Naturalization Service (INS), now U.S. Citizenship for Immigration Service (USCIS). This strategy, if successful, could serve as a model for communities throughout the city.

One last detail remained to be decided. Some in the CLC thought that the community could itself strike and then enforce a bargain with the employers. Some of these were wary of unions generally and oriented more to the independent workers' center paradigm. Others were simply concerned that the community organizing aspect of the campaign might be diminished were a union to be brought in. The prevailing view, however, was that workers needed the power and resources of a union if they were to engage their employers and achieve a legally enforceable collective bargaining agreement. It was time to pitch the campaign to Ernesto Jofre and Local 169.

## UNITE Local 169

This was a union CLC activists could feel comfortable with. Long a champion of low-wage immigrant workers, it was led by Jofre, a labor activist from Chile who had been imprisoned for three years by the Pinochet regime before being exiled to the United States in 1978. It helped also that the union's offices were convenient to the area targeted by CLC. Through the early months of 1998, CLC members had met regularly with Jofre to discuss possible organizing efforts. In the meetings, he had stressed that workers would be welcomed into the union regardless of their immigration status or the size of their employer (many unions, for bottom-line reasons, spurn the very idea of organizing small shops). He was waiting only for the CLC to find an entrée to the workers. Now AMAT was aboard and he was listening.

## Out to Brighton Beach

In conversations AMAT and CLC held with workers employed at greengrocers around the city, many workers expressed a strong desire to join a union that could raise their wages and provide protection from employer abuse and unfair treatment. In the Brighton Beach section of Brooklyn, AMAT had already organized to the extent that workers there seemed ready to move. Although eager to try out the community-labor strategy on their home turf, CLCers made the trek out to Brooklyn to lend a hand. Soon Local 169 joined the effort, and in August, Dominguez was hired as a full-time organizer. In time, as the campaign expanded into other areas of the city, additional Mexican activists, including Manuel Guerrero, were hired and trained as labor organizers.

For now the target was a ten-block stretch along Brighton Beach Avenue, with its population made up largely of recent Russian émigrés who frequented about twenty large and small Korean-owned greengroceries.

From August to November 1998, Local 169 ran a campaign to sign up workers. Hundreds of workers met with union organizers, CLC members, and other supporters to discuss the campaign. Workers had to be convinced that it would improve their conditions and that they would not face the threat of deportation. On any given night, dozens of workers met with organizers on street corners, at local diners, and in the homes of Mexican workers in the neighborhood. More than 75 percent of some five hundred workers, and a majority in every store along the corridor, signed union recognition cards indicating that they wanted their employers to recognize the union and bargain collectively for a contract. With a majority of workers signed up, the union presented the cards to the employers and called for elections, which were held in the winter of 1998. Once employers discovered this support for unionization, they hired union-busting law firms to oppose the organizing effort. Employers fired workers who led the drive and intimidated others to end their support for unionization. In addition, employers immediately raised wages to comply with federal and state wage and hour laws. Wages rose dramatically, from about $2.50 an hour to more than $5.00, and employers promised to comply with government minimums in the future. This employer carrot-and-stick approach effectively ended the campaign in Brighton Beach.

Some workers considered the effort a success once wages increased and working conditions were improved. With National Labor Relations Board (NLRB) protections so ineffective in defending the rights of workers—particularly immigrant workers—to organize into unions of their choice, the campaign was unable to convince workers that they could successfully defend their interests against the employers. Even the strongest supporters of the union could not convince their coworkers to vote the union in. The Brighton Beach drive, though successful in increasing wages—at least temporarily—demonstrated the futility of holding NLRB elections when employers are able to intimidate workers. Though many local residents supported the campaign and CLC members held protests twice weekly, there was no grassroots community organizing or sustained boycott that could pressure the owners to recognize the union. Once the drive ended, wages dropped to their previous level.

## Back on the Lower East Side

Even during the Brighton Beach drive, efforts had continued on the Lower East Side. Union organizers continued their work among greengrocery workers while CLC activists built support among church groups and community-based organizations. In the fall of 1998 a parade of over two hundred people, led by a mariachi band, marched from Charas/El Bohio to every greengrocer in the neighborhood. The idea was to put employers on notice and show workers that they had the community's support and that of the several elected officials who marched that day.

On the Lower East Side it was decided to forgo NLRB elections and instead demand employer recognition and bargaining upon demonstrating that a majority of workers had signed union cards. It was felt that community boycott lines could pressure employers to accede to that demand while at the same time protect workers from reprisals.

By late spring, a majority of the 125 workers employed at seventeen greengroceries had signed union recognition cards with Local 169. On May 1, CLC held a rally and march to protest working conditions in the stores and demand union recognition. Over three hundred workers, community residents, and elected officials joined the march, again led by a mariachi band, again stopping at each of the stores. CLC and the union invited the owners to a meeting at the local Boys Club, but only one owner and a representative of the Soho–Greenwich Village Korean Merchants Association attended. A second invitation was totally ignored. The letter of invitation had explained that the campaign wished to deal with the stores as a unit and negotiate a neighborhood-wide agreement (ensuring the stores' economic viability and including union recognition to protect workers' gains), so that no store unilaterally complying with the labor laws would be put at a competitive disadvantage. CLC indicated that if serious negotiations toward a union contract were not begun, boycotts against the stores would be initiated.

The first boycott was begun in late June 1999 at two stores on lower Avenue A—Graceland, a greengrocery, and Gracefully, a gourmet food shop. The same family owned both stores, as well as a third, Adinah's Farms, on Avenue C at Second Street. The hope was that the owners could soon be brought to the table and that an agreement responsive to the needs of workers, owners, and the community could be arrived at. Instead, the owners dug in their heels and resorted to union-busting tactics. They blasted loud music at protesters, printed slanderous leaflets identifying CLC and the union with the mafia and with the drug dealers who had once occupied the corner, and on one occasion sent four goons in a limousine to physically threaten protesters. On several occasions customers assaulted protesters or tried, unsuccessfully, to provoke violence from the boycott line. In mid-August, workers at Adinah's went on strike when they were illegally fired for supporting the union drive. A majority of workers there had signed union cards with Local 169, which after the firings filed an unfair labor practice charge with the NLRB. The campaign was expanded on October 25 when a consumer boycott line was initiated at Seventh Street Fruit and Vegetable, a store on First Avenue owned by a Lebanese immigrant family. By late summer 1999 the campaign had received substantial media coverage (in the *New York Times*, *New York Newsday*, *El Diario*, *The Villager*, and other papers as well as on several television stations).

An element essential to the campaign's success was the effort to lobby government agencies to enforce wage and hour laws. CLC and Local 169 appealed to the U.S. Department of Labor and to New York State Attorney General Eliot Spitzer. By December 1999 the Department of Labor had issued judgments for back wages against Adinah's, and the attorney general's office had launched a citywide investigation of the industry.

The coalition organized daily leafleting at the stores, particularly between 4 and 7 P.M.—cutting deeply into sales. The pressure brought to bear by consumers in the neighborhood shielded the workers from reprisals by their employers.

In December 1999, after six months of community boycotts and the perseverance of the workers on strike at Adinah's Farms, the owners finally agreed to recognize Local 169 and agreed to a contract at Adinah's. At Graceland and Gracefully an agreement was signed that guaranteed the owners' neutrality in union elections. Daniel Lucas (1999), a worker at Adinah's Farms, said of the victory:

> We have shown other workers in this industry that this can be done. I know that all store managers treat workers the way they treat us. The strike was the only way to show our power and to put pressure on the company. Now that we have won I feel proud. There are so many workers who are afraid. They can see that we are not afraid and that we won our strike.

By the winter of 2000, two other stores in the neighborhood—Fuji Apple and Hee II Market, both on First Avenue—quickly had agreed to sign contracts. By two months later a total of six stores on the Lower East Side had signed agreements with the union. These improvements in wages and working conditions have raised wages for workers in other stores throughout the neighborhood, and indeed throughout the city, as owners try to avoid being targeted. The campaign also received ongoing support from Manhattan members of the New York City Council, led by Margarita López, which held hearings on wages and working conditions in the industry.

**Korean Employers Association**

Throughout the greengrocery organizing campaign, CLC and Local 169 have encouraged Korean storeowners to form an employers' association that would recognize the union and bargain collectively on behalf of employers in the produce industry. This effort was made at the inception of the campaign and continued as it expanded throughout New York City. The idea is that, rather than organizing and bargaining store-by-store, it is better to solve the problem of illegally low wages and substandard working conditions by reaching an industry-wide master agreement. This, of course, requires having most of the workers sign union cards. By the spring of 2000, efforts in that direction had begun. Mexican workers throughout the city had become aware that they were owed back wages for years of being underpaid and were flowing into the Local 169 union hall to join the union and seek back pay.

By the summer of 2000, Attorney General Spitzer had concluded that not one store of the dozens he had investigated was in compliance with minimum wage laws. Even the owners admitted that the laws have been ignored for many years, alleging only that most stores are now paying the minimum hourly wage. Because they have voluntarily raised wages, the owners claim they do not require oversight from the union. Workers' testimony in many instances contradicts the contention that wages have been raised to legal levels, and even where they have, the experience in Brighton Beach suggests that such raises will not be permanent in the absence of a union contract. Unfortunately, although the union and CLC have expressed the hope that employers will recognize the workers' right to organize, the Korean owners remained divided.

## The Fifth Avenue Campaign

An effort to expand the campaign beyond its promising beginning on the Lower East Side began with the organization of workers at three stores in central Greenwich Village in the immediate vicinity of Local 169 headquarters. The three stores, all on Fifth Avenue, cater heavily to office workers in the area and employ two to three times as many workers as even the largest of the Lower East Side stores. The initial target was Valentino Market, a gourmet deli at Thirteenth Street, where a three-day community boycott led to union recognition and shortly thereafter a collective bargaining agreement. Meanwhile, despite early signs of co-operation, the effort to gain recognition from the Han family, owners of three large markets—East Natural and Abbigail's on the Fifth Avenue corridor and Soho Natural further downtown—became a major struggle as the owners hired a union-busting law firm to resist the organizing drive. Though nearly all the workers had signed union recognition cards, the owners refused to accept them as evidence of support for the union. Instead, they immediately raised wages and threatened workers with firing if they supported Local 169. Since the overwhelming majority of the twenty or so workers employed at East Natural supported the union, the local called for an election. However, that request was withdrawn, when better-paid, quasi-managerial employees were transferred to East Natural from the other stores, effectively packing the bargaining unit in favor of management.

Thus, CLC and Local 169 became embroiled in a dispute that continues. Though some community members were committed to maintaining the boycott lines, the situation required building alliances with workers' rights groups beyond the Lower East Side. The boycott lines were expanded and staffed primarily by Mexican immigrants, most of them members of AMAT. Newfound support also came from students at two area universities—New York University and New School University.

With worker support, the boycott lines were expanded to include all three stores owned by the Han family. Their union-busting tactics included making two separate attempts to bring in unions that would sign sweetheart deals or no contract at all. In July 2000, CLC members went to Abbigail's to inform the owners that boycott lines were being set up that day. While there, they witnessed a manager giving workers union cards from a Brooklyn-based non-AFL-CIO union. Then, in October, the Han family formed an association of employers who meant to block serious unionization efforts. The employers brought in International Longshoremen's Association (ILA) Local 1964 from Jersey City and signed recognition agreements at East Natural and several other stores. Local 1964 has publicly admitted that a primary goal was to stop the consumer boycotts. The contracts signed by the local were negotiated without the support or knowledge of the workers. This effort to create a company-dominated union was challenged by Local 169, CLC, and the workers. At a hearing held in Washington in January 2001, the AFL-CIO ruled that ILA Local 1964 is not the legitimate representative of workers at East Natural Market and that Local 169 retains the right to organize workers there.

The evidence established that UNITE's strategic campaign to organize greengrocers and the combination of tactics used under the plan have proven successful in a number of locations. With this proceeding resolved and only one union in the picture, UNITE stands a reasonable chance of consolidating its support and winning representation of East Natural employees (AFL-CIO 2001).

Workers at another store nominally represented by Local 1964—Jin Market, a Tribeca greengrocer that employs about twenty-five workers—

have signed cards with Local 169 and wear baseball caps at work indicating their support. In mid-January, CLC threw up a boycott line at the store, which was honored by a majority of residents and workers in the neighborhood. On February 20, the AFL-CIO concluded that UNITE Local 169 has the right to organize workers at Jin Market for the purpose of reaching a collective bargaining agreement despite the existence of a contract between the ILA local and the owners.

## Citywide Mobilization and Organizing

By March 2001 the greengrocery organizing campaign had gone citywide. Thousands of workers were streaming in to Local 169 headquarters to sign union recognition cards and, with the help of union lawyers and a team of law students, file back-wage claims against their employers. What started in June 1999 as a campaign to organize immigrant greengrocery workers on the Lower East Side has captured the attention of Mexican workers throughout the city. The dramatic success of these organizing efforts has emboldened these workers to sign recognition cards calling for unionization, testify for back wages at the attorney general's office, and build on the early success of the campaign.

The Korean owners continue to debate whether they should recognize workers' demands for union recognition and negotiate as a group with worker representatives and Local 169. CLC and the union continued to explore ways of educating owners on workplace standards and the rights of workers, but maintain that the first step is the recognition of the rights of workers to assemble, organize, and join the union of their choice—rights guaranteed by the Thirteenth Amendment and statutory law but flouted regularly by employers.

## Conclusion

This campaign has demonstrated the power of community-labor collaboration. With increasing numbers of undocumented immigrant workers now convinced that they can defeat their employers and demand their rights in the workplace, prospects for building a broader movement for worker rights become suddenly brighter. At the beginning, the greengrocery campaign was disparaged by many labor leaders as being a waste of resources. They believed it could not succeed in mobilizing workers in large numbers, since the stores were small and dispersed throughout the city. They also believed that immigrant Mexican workers were too vulnerable and intimidated to join the effort.

The potential of this effort is enormous. Greengrocery workers throughout New York City have already improved their conditions, and the organizing drive is poised to bring thousands of new members into the union movement. The campaign has demonstrated to new immigrant workers from Mexico that the union movement cares about them and that they can advance their interests through organizing. The campaign is also testimony to the capacity of community members to effect change for people who work among them. In the new economy, work is conducted in public, not inside closed factory gates, making it easier for community residents concerned with workers' rights to pressure employers to treat their workers fairly. The consumer boycott has proven an effective mechanism to defend workers against employer abuse. In a seemingly cynical world, the greengrocery organizing effort has shown that most people indeed have a social conscience and, when given the opportunity, will take a stand with those willing to fight for basic human rights and justice in the workplace.

## 5

SARU JAYARAMAN AND IMMANUEL NESS

# Models of Worker Organizing

Over the last century, labor strategists have proposed and employed a range of approaches to organize and mobilize workers to improve working conditions and build power to challenge employer domination over the workplace. A litany of strategies has appeared, disappeared, and re-appeared—each held up at different moments as the correct method of organizing. As membership and density in the organized labor movement have declined since 1955—a decline that has accelerated in the last two decades—new organizing strategies have again proliferated among trade unionists and labor organizers. In the early 1990s, debates in the AFL-CIO focused attention on labor segments ripe for organizing as a means of increasing union density and power. National unions have targeted industries seen as ready for organizing across the U.S. in much the same way as local unions have searched for suitable local labor market segments and "hot shops."

John Sweeney's election as president of the AFL-CIO in 1995 kicked off a concerted organizing drive targeting low-wage and immigrant workers who replaced previous generations of white workers in manufacturing and who today make up a large part of the service sector. Approaches to organizing varied. National unions were most interested in targeting new industrial labor market segments to gain greater market share and have greater leverage over wages and working conditions. The idea behind this new approach is to focus on key industrial sectors rather than organizing an assortment of labor markets. To wit, several of the unions in the Unite to Win Coalition that broke away from the AFL-CIO in the summer of 2005 have focused on key industries. The Service Employees International Union (SEIU) has concentrated on health care and custodial workers, and UNITE-HERE, once organizers of garment and textile workers and restaurants, focuses on industrial laundries and large hotels and cafeterias. But the AFL-CIO has not succeeded in convincing most other national unions to employ industrial strategies. As a result, most unions are content to maintain market share in their industries or, at best, to reach out to new workers in those industries.

The AFL-CIO stressed building alliances with local community groups and religious institutions as well as across local unions, but this emphasis did not seem to mesh with national industrial organizing strategies. National unions instead acted as "field marshals," devising policies and directing the work of typically outside organizers. This can clearly be seen in the AFL-CIO Organizing Institute's emphasis on hiring college students to put programs into motion locally. In many instances such efforts burned out new organizers without building local worker leadership or power.

Despite the weakness in training strong local leadership, the strategy nonetheless proved successful for some national unions. The SEIU Justice for Janitors national organizing campaign, initiated in the late 1980s, targeted the mostly immigrant custodial workforce working in commercial buildings that outsourced cleaning services to independent contractors. Under the new approach, unions seek to gain employer recognition outside of the National Labor Relations Board (NLRB), which is seen as a toothless agency that does not work and in effect prevents workers from organizing. Such unions have successfully leveraged power through utilizing militant approaches—walkouts, boycotts, recognition strikes, and other forms of concerted activity not seen since the 1940s. However, a downside to this industrial approach is that these unions typically employ top-down organizing, from time to time raiding other unions inside and outside the AFL-CIO or negotiating substandard bargaining agreements in the desperate search for increased membership. Typically, national unions exercise authority over member union locals and unaffiliated workers organizing and building independent power.

## The IWW Approach to Organizing

The Industrial Workers of the World (IWW), long seen as a relic of the past, today appears to have an innovative approach to organizing workers that differs markedly from most AFL-CIO organizing efforts. The IWW's organizing strategy seems appropriate for the new nonstandard contingent workforce that has expanded so rapidly in the contemporary era. The IWW model does not view gaining recognition and reaching collective bargaining agreements with employers as the preferred outcome. Rather, this approach stresses the importance of autonomous worker organizing with the goal of building rank-and-file solidarity and power to prod management into improving wages and conditions—an approach that is now being increasingly adopted by some unions.

Formed in 1905, the IWW saw employer recognition as anathema—a form of conciliation since workers would eventually be co-opted and marginalized by the capitalist system. Throughout the first two decades of the twentieth century, the IWW employed radical organizing strategies that became the basis for the radical workers' movement in the 1930s and 1940s. The IWW approach was frequently successful in organizing workers in the short run, but could not address the problem of consolidating power to institutionalize the gains won by workers. The strategy was clearly preferable to the autocratic traditional union approach that robs most workers of independence and eventually weakens the union. On the other hand, the IWW—adamantly opposed to the capitalist system—would not agree to long-term agreements that bound workers to employers. But the approach of organizing rank-and-file power without building an enduring structure or organization intensifies the problem of consolidating past worker gains. The problem remains: How can worker power be consolidated without ongoing organization? The answer to this dilemma remains elusive.

Labor activist and lawyer Staughton Lynd (1996) asserts that more limited forms of "workplace contractualism," a defining characteristic of CIO unionism, should be explored as an alternative. "I think it is very important to avoid approaching contractualism in a fetishistic manner. That is, the critical question is not whether or not to have a contract. The critical question is what is in the contract. Ninety-nine percent of AFL-CIO contracts contain a no-strike clause, whereby labor gives up its self-activity, and a management prerogative clause, whereby management retains its ability to act unilaterally, for instance in closing plants. No contract is better than such a contract." Lynd posits a third way: "If workers can find a way to achieve gains through concerted activity without a contract, then when they enter into contracts, those contracts can be simple agreements as to what need not be fought over at the moment, and above all, they can be agreements that do not surrender the right to strike or acknowledge the right to close the plant."

## Models of Organizing

We now examine the similarities and differences between union and nonunion organizing models that have evolved in the last two decades.

### *The Old Organizing Model*

Under the traditional model of union organizing that has been in place for over half a century, employer recognition and collective bargaining leading to a contract remains an integral feature of the labor movement's strategy. However, this model has been unsuccessful due to national labor law, which allows employers to avoid unions through a host of tactics not envisioned when the National Labor Relations Act was passed in 1935. Within the unorganized labor market, the traditional union recognition model is based on organizing members at a specific facility for a union election. A union can call for an election by demonstrating that at least one-third of the workers in a shop support the union. If the union gains cards from more than 50 percent of the workers, the employer may then accept the card count and begin to bargain with the union.

Typically, however, employers call for elections to contest the union presence as a means of retaining control over workers. If the union succeeds in winning a majority in an election monitored by the NLRB, the employer is obligated to recognize the union as the exclusive bargaining representative for all the workers in a shop. Upon the union's winning the election, the employer is mandated to bargain in good faith with union representatives for the purposes of signing an agreement stipulating the terms and conditions of employment. Due to the failure of national labor law to protect workers, national unions seeking to increase membership have jettisoned the election process and instead tried to gain recognition on the basis of the card count alone. Still, the law frequently allows employers to successfully resist the union by stalling in contract negotiations and calling an impasse. Upon impasse, employers then may implement a contract without the participation of the union or workers.

### *Reaching Out to Nonunion Workers*

As national labor law has failed traditional unions and as union density plummeted in the 1980s, the AFL-CIO conceived the Union Benefit Membership Program in an effort to target workers employed in nonunion jobs in industries where unions had lost significant market share. The program was adopted by several national unions, which initiated associate membership targeted to appeal to workers in their industries who were not unionized. The goal of the program was to engender a positive image of the specific union—and unions in general—among workers.

Typically, national union associate membership programs were aimed at nonunion workers who would not otherwise have access to health and insurance benefits, in specific industrial categories in which the unions had regular members. Many of these workers formed part of the restructured new economy that includes a rapidly growing contingent labor force that does not receive benefits through their jobs. These associate membership programs usually featured a general package of limited benefits, including the Union Benefit Membership Program, which provided nonunion workers with access to general benefits such as a credit card, limited legal assistance, and sometimes the right to buy into a health plan.

### The Workers Center

Workers centers were developed in the mid-1980s as a means to train, assist, and mobilize workers in low-wage industries. Most workers centers sought to organize the growing immigrant population not represented by unions. Whether union-based or independent (nonunion), workers centers typically provide the same services. The major difference is the objectives of the centers. Union-based workers centers are motivated by the prospects of signing up new workers, gaining recognition agreements with employers, and successfully negotiating toward collective bargaining agreements. Even though members of the workers centers are not union members, the end result of the process for unions is increased support of organizing efforts for the purpose of employer recognition and contract negotiation.

Most independent workers centers are not motivated by the prospect of achieving recognition and contracts from employers; rather, their primary aim is to educate and organize workers to demand improved conditions on the job. These centers sometimes refer workers to unions, but this is not their main purpose. Some members come to lodge complaints of poor working conditions, violations of wage and hour laws, and harassment in union shops.

## Features of Union-Based and Nonunion Workers Centers

Both union-based and independent workers centers share common features, but differ in their tactics, strategies, and goals. The three key elements are (1) education and training; (2) direct support and assistance; and (3) solidarity, organizing, and mobilization.

### *Education and Training*

Education provided by workers centers focuses on three areas: English-language instruction, labor rights education, and ideological education.

### *English-Language Instruction*

Typically, all workers centers provide basic English-language education through English as a second language (ESL) classes to workers who have trouble communicating in their new language. The vast majority of workers centers provide services to immigrants working in low-wage industries. These classes give workers the essential language skills and cultural awareness they need to survive and become productive members of their communities. Most important, fluency in English helps give workers a voice in communicating with their employers, the general public, and government agencies and nonprofits.

### *Labor Rights*

A second service of workers centers is educating people about their basic legal rights as workers in the United States. Labor rights education is especially important since most state labor agencies do not have the personnel to monitor employer compliance with wage-and-hour laws. Thus, many employers in urban regions do not comply with federal labor standards that mandate paying workers minimum wage and paying overtime to those working more than forty hours in a given week. Workers also receive education about their rights as individuals in society, including information on federal and state laws prohibiting racial and sexual discrimination on the job. Most important, workers are educated about their basic rights as workers under the National Labor Relations Act, which requires that employers allow employees to organize independently or through unions and gives workers the right to legally claim unpaid back wages.

## Ideological Education

Union and nonunion workers centers diverge in the forms of ideological education they provide to workers. Typically the key goal of union-based centers is to inculcate in workers the importance of organizing for the purpose of gaining employer recognition culminating in collective bargaining agreements. Nonunion workers centers are substantially less interested in union representation and having bargaining agreements with employers: Instead, independent workers centers are motivated by the goal of educating about class, racial, and gender inequality while inspiring workers to directly challenge this oppression by collectively organizing and mobilizing.

At workers centers where most participants are new immigrants, Paulo Freire's models of education are utilized to show workers the injustices of global inequality. The Freirian model, which teaches participants about the structures of inequality, is a common feature of independent workers centers. Through the use of images and role-playing, the goal of the Freirian model is to go beyond educational awareness of inequality and oppression, and to arouse workers to challenge the injustices they confront every day on the job, in the public sphere, and in government laws.

## Direct Support and Assistance

Workers frequently become members of independent or union-based workers centers in an attempt to find representation in wage and hour disputes with employers, and to get assistance with federal, state, and local government agencies. Legal assistance is necessary for monitoring wage and hour violations, representing workers against employers that violate minimum wage laws, seeking unpaid back wages, and monitoring workplaces to prevent sexual harassment. Typically, workers centers have labor lawyers that workers rely on for legal assistance in disputes with management, immigration advice, and family and consumer advice.

The availability of legal assistance is a vital resource for those who turn to workers centers. Thus, virtually every union and nonunion workers center provides this service to workers seeking restitution from their employers. While the undocumented immigrants who frequently join workers centers are not permitted to work in the U.S., employers are still required to comply with federal and state minimum wage laws and

other ordinances that protect all workers from discrimination and oppressive conditions. However, federal and state government authorities
rarely enforce laws protecting workers from abusive conditions, leading
workers to turn to lawyers for redress.

If providing legal assistance becomes the primary function of a workers
center, there is a risk of creating dependency of workers on staff, ne-
glecting the prime objective of organizing and mobilizing workers. As a
result, workers centers sometimes transform into the equivalent of social service agencies as a substitute for their original mission of creating
mutual aid organizations that educate workers and provide the tools for
empowerment.

## Solidarity, Organizing, and Mobilization

When workers centers supply legal assistance simply for the purpose of
providing a service to members, workers typically become dependent
on the professional assistance that helps them navigate through the system. However, if legal assistance is matched with organizing, it can be a
useful—if not necessary—method of mobilizing workers in struggles
against employers and in efforts to improve their social welfare. Workers who are organizing into synchronized social forces frequently require legal information about unlawful employer threats and abuse. Labor
lawyers are crucial for providing legal advice and representation before
federal and state departments of labor and the NLRB, in lawsuits brought
against employers for violations of worker rights, and sometimes against
unions that neglect to properly represent members.

## Union-Based and Independent Workers Center Models

Since the objectives of union-based and independent workers centers
vary, each has modeled programs differently. By analyzing each model,
one can better understand the benefits and disadvantages of the programs in advancing worker rights and improving workplace conditions.

## National Union Workers Centers

Since the late 1980s several national unions have opened workers centers of various types to recruit nonunion labor as new members into
their organizations. These centers were created primarily to organize

members for the purpose of gaining recognition and collective bargaining agreements from employers. The centers were formed in traditional labor markets in which unions had been losing density, and in new economy labor markets in cases where old union-based labor markets were in decline.

Initially, union-based workers centers were regarded as a long-term method of educating and organizing workers and gaining traction in desired labor markets. However, as organized labor has moved toward a strategy of targeting new and growing labor markets, some unions have closed workers centers serving older industries that hold little promise of recruiting new members. Some unions consider investing resources in workers centers to be costly and extraneous to their new mission. Consequently, some national unions have closed workers centers and directed resources toward top-down, hierarchical organizing that targets labor markets in which industry-wide recognition agreements and contracts can be achieved.

The leading unions that have opened workers centers are the United Farm Workers (UFW), HERE, Communications Workers of America (CWA), and UNITE. Union-based workers centers vary in form and structure, but their primary objective is to provide political and ideological support for unionization among immigrants and workers in new sectors of the economy. In retrospect, unions that operated workers centers sought unionization within a short time span. Some unions have considered workers centers too costly to justify economically if they do not help achieve employer recognition and collective bargaining agreements.

### Case Study of UNITE's Garment Workers Justice Center

A prime example of workers centers administered by a national union is the UNITE Garment Workers Justice Centers (GWJC), formed in 1994 in New York City, Miami, Los Angeles, and San Francisco. These centers provided unorganized garment workers with associate membership in the union, which entitled them to industrial skills training, English as a second language classes, human and labor rights education, and access to the Union Privilege Benefit Membership Program. Indeed, the program worked exceedingly well. By mid-1995 the New York City GWJC claimed to have organized nearly two thousand workers.

However, by the late 1990s the workers centers were closed down by the international union. In New York City's fashion district, the GWJC effectively provided educational and training services to workers, supported workers in back wage claims, and mobilized and organized workers. But the volatile and unstable New York garment industry is not amenable to gaining recognition and collective bargaining agreements with footloose employers that are capable of closing and reopening sweatshops to avoid unions and evade paying workers back wages. Due to the industry's volatility and the difficulty in gaining recognition and collective bargaining agreements, UNITE has all but abandoned organizing efforts in the regional garment industry. In the mid-1990s the union planned to mobilize garment workers for a general industry-wide strike to pressure employers for recognition—an effort that never came to fruition due primarily to the fluidity of the immigrant workforce and the ability of employers to evade the union.

Even given conditions under which workers were organized and primed for collective action, the organizing effort failed—due in part to the union's own lofty objective of gaining recognition and collective bargaining agreements with employers. The effort to organize immigrant workers by the GWJC provides evidence of the power imbalance in the garment industry, despite the fact that workers are primed for collective action and protest. In the mid-1990s, undocumented workers engaged in spontaneous work stoppages to protest low and unpaid wages and dangerous conditions. Unauthorized sit-down strikes—once a relic of 1930s and 1940s labor protests—occurred daily, despite threats of dismissal, imminent arrest, and deportation.

UNITE's efforts to organize workers typically succeeded in gaining back wages from employers, but efforts to obtain recognition and collective bargaining agreements usually failed. A case in point is a sit-down strike in December 1996 in Manhattan's Fashion District that led to petitioning for union recognition from the sweatshop's owners. The firm had habitually failed to pay workers on time—and in some cases at all—and had accumulated hundreds of thousands of dollars in outstanding claims for back wages. Workers also complained that the sweatshop imposed excessively onerous working conditions; had harassed, disrespected, and physically abused workers; and employed child labor. The sweatshop was a subcontractor that produced garments for major national and regional clothing retailers. It employed a workforce of about three hundred, mostly young, female, undocumented immigrants from Mexico and Ecuador.

After the owners refused to recognize the workers' petition to join a union, the workers in the factory initiated a sit-down strike, demanding back wages and union representation. Workers refused supervisor demands that they end the strike, until finally managers promised immediate payment of back wages. When the workers left the factory, suspected union sympathizers were interrogated, threatened with dismissal, and otherwise intimidated by sweatshop managers. Failure to get a positive response from managers prompted the workers to organize a public demonstration in the days before Christmas, targeting a large New York department store catering to trendy, upscale shoppers that was a primary customer for the sweatshop's apparel. Amid growing public awareness of the prevalence of sweatshop conditions at the factory, the demonstration was embarrassing to the department store, which canceled its order for garments subcontracted to the sweatshop.

The sweatshop finally relented and agreed to recognize the union and negotiate a contractual agreement governing wages and working conditions. The owners agreed to pay workers forty dollars per week toward back wage claims until they were paid in full. The contract also required managers to treat workers respectfully, discipline workers only with just cause, refrain from threatening and hitting workers, reduce required working hours, and provide seniority rights.

The actions taken by the sweatshop workers leading to union recognition reveal how workers may utilize their collective power to improve their conditions. The reluctant decision by the sweatshop's owners to relent and acknowledge demands for a union demonstrates that workers gained the upper hand by threatening to withhold their work and exposing the abusive conditions in the sweatshop to the public.

At face value, all the components of workers' power were present and contributed to the organizing victory. Workers demanded union recognition and payment of back wages, and threatened to withhold their work and publicly expose the sweatshop. In accepting the workers' demands, management considered the threat of a continued strike, public exposure, and the potential loss of business to be less desirable than acceding to worker demands for dignity on the job.

Seemingly, then, the political and economic system grants new immigrant workers employed in sweatshops the ability to exercise power to improve their conditions. Unfortunately, the conflict does not end there—revealing the influence of the dominant corporate powers that override worker militancy and resistance. Shortly after workers and management agreed to a new contract governing their relations, the owners failed to live up to the terms of the agreement. After the garment workers' public demonstrations, a major retailer canceled its orders for apparel produced at the sweatshop. Other retailers were reluctant to subcontract their work to the sweatshop due to the negative publicity and the lower profits they might earn if required to pay subcontractors that provide workers a living wage.

There are no state and federal regulations that prevent manufacturers from switching from one subcontractor to another. As a consequence, the sweatshop came under heavy financial pressure as a result of decisions by retailers at the top of the food chain to subcontract work to new lower-cost sweatshops. By early January the sweatshop again failed to pay workers back wages and their current weekly wages. Also, the union uncovered evidence that the sweatshop was secretly transferring work to a sweatshop in nearby Long Island City to avoid the union contract and the back wage claims while continuing to produce apparel for its regular contractors.

The power that the workers in the sweatshop thought they possessed evaporated very rapidly. First, the workers had no control in making sure that government regulatory agencies enforced laws that ban sweatshop conditions. Second, the workers had no say in the independent decisions of corporate retailers to cancel orders that provided needed jobs for low-wage workers. And third, the decision by the sweatshop to transfer work to a new facility was made independently of the workers and their union. Workers had no control over decisions by government and businesses that affected their very livelihood. Finally, the union, too, decided that the effort was hopeless, since the structure of the industry is so contrary to the interests of workers.

It is therefore fairly narrow-minded to view power as simply a dynamic between the workers and their immediate sweatshop employers. Though they had a direct voice in the decision to withhold their labor, protest against abuses, and finally reach an agreement with managers, the voice of the workers was absent in the actions and nonactions taken by individuals, organizations, and government authorities that dominate the system of production.

### Local Union Workers Centers

Local unions that have a greater level of independence from national unions frequently organize workers centers to mobilize and organize workers in discrete labor markets. These workers centers can assist workers in filing legal claims for unpaid back wages and overtime, improving wages and working conditions, and filing racial and sexual harassment complaints.

The local union hall typically functions as a drop-in center for workers in distinct industries. As with the national unions, the primary objective of local union workers centers is to gain recognition and collective bargaining contracts with employers in order to increase membership.

### Independent Workers Centers

Responding largely to traditionally neglected workforces, independent workers' centers have proliferated since the late 1980s. Most of these centers focus on specific ethnic populations, and a few organize around a specific industry. Given their focus on marginalized workers, New York City's independet workers' centers have not focused on collective bargaining agreements, but have had to respond creatively to unjust working conditions, to win legislative campaigns, and to raise public attention to the plight of immigrant workers. Depsite their small size, independent workers' centers present a unique and necessary force in New York City, raising public attention to the plight of workers in ways that unions cannot.

## Conclusion

Creating enduring worker organizations is a complex problem. Efforts to build lasting organizational power will not succeed through top-down strategies that strip workers of participation, nor can they be sustained without the growth of institutional power. Thus, our argument has three premises: (1) the imperative of worker participation in organizing; (2) long-term and continuous organizing; and (3) the formulation of strategies directed at the constantly changing nature of jobs and concomitant changes in the workforce.

### Worker Inclusion

Upon examination of an array of organizing models, we find no ideal, enduring model that encompasses all workers at all times. But no strategy will succeed without the active participation of rank-and-file workers, who retain the most crucial weapon: the strike threat and the potential to seize and shut down the workplace. If the goal is to establish recognition and collective bargaining agreements between unions and employers without the input of workers, the process will inevitably create cynicism, whereby workers regard themselves as voiceless pawns in an external power struggle over their terms and conditions of work. Most unions are motivated by the imperative of advancing worker power, but more often than not, workers are excluded and their voices are silenced.

## Organizing for the Long Term

Among the few unions that actively engage in organizing campaigns, there is great pressure to produce rapid—and at times immediate—results. This inclination leads to a failure to account for the rapidly changing historical conditions that different workers typically face on the job. By demanding immediate returns, winning over historically ignored workers—women, people of color, and new immigrants—is an exceedingly difficult task, even if unions gain recognition and a contract. Unions must win over workers first. It is a monumental mistake to consider workers as supporters when they are not included—and one that will inevitably lead to the perception of unions as third parties. Employer antiunion campaigns appeal to this notion of unions as outside dues collectors, an image perpetuated by the reality that a not insignificant percentage of union contracts are in essence protection agreements that keep workers from self-organizing for improved wages and working conditions. Despite this distressing reality, it is a remarkable fact that the vast majority of low-wage workers support unionization. But organizing can never be considered a short-term project. Why should workers trust a union that parachutes in organizers from the national office for a short-term organizing campaign? Some national unions have built successful relationships with workers by fighting alongside them in long-term battles. HERE's fourteen-year-long battle for union recognition at the Frontier Hotel in Las Vegas is an important case in point, and one that built the reputation of the national union and turned the city into a "union town" by the late 1990s.

## Multiple Strategies

Our third premise is that different workplaces require unique ways of thinking about how to mobilize workers in order to challenge employer domination. There is no such thing as a "one size fits all" approach in which organizing models are imposed on local unions and workers without consideration of the unique conditions workers face every day on the job. For example, the organization of workers in automobile assembly plants in the 1930s and 1940s necessitated markedly different approaches and tactics than those used in organizing restaurant workers today.

## 6

Saru Jayaraman

# La Alianza Para La Justicia: A Team Approach to Immigrant Worker Organizing

In their book *The Miner's Canary*, Lani Guinier and Gerald Torres describe the concept of "power-with"—the importance of leadership by an affected community in a struggle for justice that primarily impacts them but affects others as well.[1] As Guinier and Torres describe, community members should lead because they know the struggle better than anyone else and are more motivated to fight it. Members are the best organizers; they know the community, its political landscape, and its human assets better than anyone. Most important, only if members lead their own struggle will the struggle continue long after the outsiders (often white, often professionals—organizers and lawyers) leave. This concept has long been used by community and labor organizers as the chosen means for achieving justice; its underlying premise will serve as the framework for discussing lawyering, organizing, and leadership development in this chapter.

In this chapter, we will draw upon the experiences and wisdom of three Latino immigrant worker leaders to first discuss some of the problems encountered by using traditional legal services as part of a social justice movement, particularly for immigrant workers, and then to describe a new organizing model instituted at the Workplace Project, a Latino immigrant worker organizing center based in Long Island, New York.[2] In particular, we will outline the process we underwent to develop and implement the model, the model's potential for organizing workers for power in situations where traditional union organizing simply will not work, and its drawbacks and failures in such organizing efforts. Most important, we will study the model's ability to build true power among immigrant workers by helping them develop complex leadership skills that necessarily relate to aspects of their life other than work. We assert that the problem with most traditional legal services is that they create dependency and isolation among workers, preventing them from leading their own struggle, and that avoiding such pitfalls requires developing leadership that is genuine and holistic.

**Problems with the Legal Clinic**

In the fall of 1999, the staff of the Workplace Project[3] decided to study new models of combining law and organizing so that the organization could better follow the "power-with" model. In particular, the organization sought to genuinely meet its mission of organizing Latino immigrant workers for better working conditions. A small committee of staff members began a process of studying various models of law and organizing, meeting with staff, board, and worker members around various ideas. It became clear, particularly from workers' experiences in the clinic, that group problem-solving was necessary. Thus, we created La Alianza Para La Justicia (the Alliance for Justice), a new law and organizing program that succeeded in tripling the numbers of workers that stayed involved with the organizing efforts.

Both board and staff members of the Workplace Project had identified two major problems, symptomatic of many legal services programs, with the center's existing model of providing legal services as a way of attracting new members into the ongoing organizing campaigns. First, the workers had grown increasingly dependent on lawyers to solve their problems. Second, workers were isolated from other workers in resolving their cases, both in their own workplace and in the organization. As a result of this dependency creation and worker isolation, the Workplace Project's clinic was not ultimately contributing to the organizing efforts; workers would often receive their legal services, perhaps take the workers' rights course, and leave without ever having joined an organizing campaign.

*Creating Dependency*

Nearly all lawyers and many organizers face the risk of creating dependence on their services among community members, thus preventing a community from autonomously asserting itself, building true power, and winning long-term change. Because the legal profession has erected an illusion of unattainable knowledge around the legal system, there is an assumption that only lawyers can speak the legal language and advocate for the underrepresented within the system, and that workers cannot advocate for themselves. As Maria Claribel Perez, leader of the factory workers' team, states, one major problem is that "we do not know that as workers we can defend ourselves."

For example, in his reflections on serving as a clinical professor at NYU's School of Law, Richard Marisco describes his legal clinic's experiences working with the "ARA," a grassroots organization that grew out of a low-income community of color that sought to fight bank redlining.[4] The clinic's attorneys and law students began to do much of ARA's work, and this did not leave room for ARA board members to take leadership or responsibility; when there was no longer a staff person present, rather than board members taking the lead, Marisco did. Thus, board members became less and less involved, until the ARA dissolved altogether.[5] Marisco's honest self-evaluation reveals a dangerous phenomenon of legal representation: If a lawyer handles everything for the client without giving her the opportunity to take leadership within the case, when future problems arise she will believe that she is not able to solve the problem on her own.

Of course, the Workplace Project did not have a typical legal services program. Housed in an organizing center, the attorney always emphasized organizing and consistently encouraged workers to bring in coworkers. Nevertheless, the relationship between the attorney and the group of workers was almost entirely a legal one. Maria Claribel Perez, leader of the factory workers' team of La Alianza, notes that the issue of dependence on lawyers was a major problem that existed with the legal clinic at the Workplace Project previously.

> [W]hen the legal clinic existed, or just one person helping the workers, it was like the workers' problems were the responsibility of that one person. The clinic did not give the worker the opportunity to learn or really know their rights for themselves. And having a clinic like that created the situation where the worker arrived looking for a solution to her problem, and afterward disappeared. Therefore, the change to the other model was very important because it gave the workers the opportunity to be able to organize, and at the same time, those same workers would be able to find solutions to their own problems. The most important thing, I believe, is that in each case, it is not an attorney who has to seek the solution, but it

is the workers themselves, using their own knowledge, who will do so. For example, the workers themselves continue learning about their rights in this country, and that as workers they have the opportunity to better themselves and learn many things. (Perez 2001)

Perez goes on to explain why breaking the cycle of dependency is so important.

> When one has experienced so many problems that happened in the past, one also begins to see that it has happened not to one person but to so many people, one becomes very angry and indignant, and says, "No, I have to do something, we have to do something together, so that we can defend ourselves." We have to do something ourselves, because one day no one will be there to say, "I will help you." (Perez 2001)

Similar to Perez, Ron Chisom, community organizer, denounced the situation in which a lawyer too quickly becomes the dominant leader within a community group, in an interview with Loyola University School of Law professor William P. Quigley. Chisom attributes this phenomenon to the workers' view of the lawyer, and not the lawyer's view of herself. "The lawyer ends up almost as a god to the group, and that will kill off the momentum and emotionalism that brought the group that far. The people lose interest as the lawyer becomes the momentum. The lawyer can stimulate the group, pacify the group, or walk out at any time. This effectively kills the leadership and power of the group . . . the collective power of the group is transferred from the individuals to the lawyer."[6]

### Relying on the Legal Rights Framework Leads to Worker Isolation

The Workplace Project's legal clinic consistently encouraged organizing. Workers were allowed to meet with the attorney only after they had met with an organizer and were required to take an eight-week workers' rights course that was to inspire them into organizing. Nevertheless, when they did meet with the attorney, primarily legal strategies were used in most cases.

According to Miami professor of law Anthony Alfieri, public interest lawyers "give" people their legal rights and "take" from them a sense of autonomy and independence.[7] This phenomenon is due in large part to the fact that telling people their legal rights limits the choices people have to effect change within their lives. For example, many workers come to the Workplace Project with complaints of unjust firings. Due to New York State's Employment-at-Will legislation, in the legal clinic workers would be told that legally there was little they could do. Although organizing against the discriminatory employer who fired the employee might have been suggested, there was no structure for these workers to actually carry out the organizing around an unjust firing. Thus, the message to workers was that there was not much that could be done—in other words, since the legal strategy would not work, there was no way to fight the injustice. Thus, justice itself becomes defined by legal strategies. NYU School of Law professor Gerald Lopez describes this phenomenon in his book *Rebellious Lawyering.*

> As [many] lawyers see it, subordinated people generally accept their positions in this life and live accordingly, or at least they fight ineffectually when left principally to their own devices. The legal system mystifies them; it hoodwinks them into believing in its legitimacy and into accepting as right and just (if not "natural") the world as it is. This perceived state of affairs unfortunately leaves it to the lawyer alone to challenge (*for* the subordinated client) the ordering of daily and imagined life, through strategies the lawyer presumes are alien to the client's way of understanding and operating. . . . This self-perceived dilemma and the work it perpetuates reflects a failing common to many lawyers of all sorts: they too often ignore and trivialize the practices through which clients already work to control their lives.[8]

One of the direct consequences of privileging legal methods over others, and thus maintaining a primarily legal relationship between lawyer and worker, is that the worker ends up being isolated from other workers who have similar problems. Although the Workplace Project's legal clinic required that workers take a workers' rights course in order to receive the services (a group setting), the fact that cases were being dealt with through a mostly legal relationship meant that workers were isolated from other workers in the process of resolving their problems, or "cases." Workers might be encouraged to bring in fellow workers from their workplace to make their cases stronger, but there was no structured program to assist the worker in doing so. This isolation made collective power more difficult to develop over time. As Eduardo Platero, leader of the custodial workers' team, explains, the team approach of La Alianza ended up being more effective in the long run.

La Alianza worked well because with this model we are able to know more about one another as workers, we have more ideas as a group. La Alianza helped us use our own experiences and knowledge to inform what we were doing. What worked best was the support of our fellow workers, having so many people supporting one another, instead of one person helping everyone. This also gave us more credibility with the union. When we were writing letters to the union, it gave us more power to have the signatures of many workers. It also worked so that all the workers had the liberty to share their problems with one another, so we could know each others' concerns deeply. (Platero 2002)

## La Alianza: A New Model for Collective Power

### The Process of Developing a New Model

These problems with the Workplace Project's legal clinic had been discussed in meetings and retreats with staff, board directors, and members for several years. Often in these meetings, staff and members would reach a consensus around the need to somehow change the legal program to better meet the Workplace Project's mission of *organizing* Latino immigrant workers to fight exploitation in the workplace.

After speaking with staff, board, workers, and volunteers, we[9] put together an initial plan in which workers entering the Workplace Project for the first time would attend a group workshop in which they would share their particular workplace legal problem with other workers, learn about their rights, and be invited to join an industry team. They would be told openly about the problems we had with the previous model and the need for workers to solve problems for themselves, collectively, without depending on lawyers. They would join teams in one of three industries—factories, restaurants, and custodial work—that were comprised of workers from the same industry, volunteers, students, and an attorney/organizer. Workers in the teams would first help one another recruit fellow workers from the various workplaces represented in the team, then strategize and act together around each of the members' workplace problems, using both organizing and legal strategies. Every three months team members would be offered a one-and-a-half-day course on organizing, from which they could graduate and become members of the Workplace Project. Team participation and the organizing course thus replaced the old eight-week workers' rights course as member entry for many workers.

As opposed to the previous model, where they would start organizing only after they had taken an eight-week workers' rights course and received some amount of legal services, workers were organizing from the moment they got involved, and kept organizing throughout the process. Workers in La Alianza never experienced any form of a service relationship, even though their needs were still addressed. For example, Jose Canales Chicas explains the development of the restaurant workers' team.

> When I arrived at the Workplace Project, it was for a labor problem . . . I came and got involved, even though my workplace problem always continued being a problem. But I started adapting myself to the ways of the Workplace Project. I understood the commitment I needed to make to help the other workers with their problems. Through the [orientation] workshop, I understood the commitment I needed to make to be with a team. In the beginning [our team] was only two people, but more people joined the team over time. We organized the group, and decided, instead of calling it "restaurant workers' team" . . . to call it another name—VER (Venceremos Empleados de Restaurantes—Restaurant Workers Will Succeed). . . . Our mission is to organize people, to conscientize them, so that the group grows. We even had t-shirts made, with monograms that said, "Venceremos Empleados de Restaurantes." (Chicas 2001)

Similarly, Perez describes the growth of the factory workers' team.

> When we arrived our team consisted of no more than three or four persons, but as we were a group that worked together, everyone for everyone, not simply services for one person, we began to work together in a united way. We began to look for ideas and solutions, and think about what we could do to reach out to more workers, to bring more people into the group, and at the same time seek solutions to the problems that the workers in the group had. And with time, for example, more friends arrived, former coworkers, from the same workplaces where we had been. We began to distribute cards and flyers all over the place, to let people know about our group, and that there existed a Center for the workers. In that way, little by little, we began to have more people in the group, and the people also began to gain more trust in our group, and kept coming to the Workplace Project. But at the beginning it was very difficult (even now it is difficult) to convince people and speak to them about what the group does and what the Workplace Project does. Nevertheless, we have succeeded [in convincing some workers to join], and little by little the

group continues to improve, and we have succeeded in having many members. Perhaps some come with [legal] problems, but others come simply because they have learned what the group is and does, and have stayed because they like to help others who have problems. (Perez 2001)

Of course, La Alianza was not developed and implemented without a yearlong struggle to convince members, board, and staff that workers, in fact, were capable of advocating for themselves and one another without a lawyer leading the charge. In their book *The Miner's Canary*, Guinier and Torres use the Workplace Project's immigrant worker board of directors as an example of "power-with." Without consciousness raising about the problems with traditional lawyering, however, the Workplace Project's Latino immigrant worker board members sometimes reflected some of the same preferences for lawyers that exist in mainstream society. Thus, this board was resistant to the idea of workers learning to resolve problems on their own, without relying on a lawyer. To address this issue, we used a series of role plays to explain the need for the new model to board and staff. Clearly, "power-with" is not the easy task of simply putting workers on a board or in the front of the room. It involves a long, complex process of leadership development, politicization, and continual reassessment by the members themselves of the power dynamics within the institution.

### Potential for Group Support Where Union Organizing May Not Work

The workers consistently cited the La Alianza's provision of mutual support among team members as the best aspect of the model.

What worked about the model [La Alianza] was the unity, the strength, the union that is created when a group of people who are suffering the same pain work together (instead of simply having one person, like an attorney, help everyone). The model is not only for one person, but involves mutual support among all group members. It is not individual, but always in group mode. The major benefit of the model was that it created an organized group for more strength. (Chicas 2001)

Chicas and other workers would often talk about the fact that the teams provided them with support that they could never find among coworkers. This was particularly significant because the teams were often organizing workers in workplaces where union organizing was difficult or unlikely. For example, Chicas knew that the various small restaurants, delis, and fast-food operations represented in his team might never be considered by a union (based on a few unsuccessful attempts to invite a union into a restaurant). Thus, it was significant to the workers who could not find support among their fellow workers, and would never have the support of a union, that they found structured support—and collective power—among other restaurant workers at the Workplace Project.

In several instances, workers who could not find support among fellow workers also did not have the support of their union. In many of these situations, traditional union-organizing tactics—forming a committee, calling mass workplace meetings during lunch, sneaking into workplaces to reach out to more workers—simply would not work. Workers who came to us complaining about an unresponsive union often had already been labeled the troublemakers in their workplaces before coming to us, and were avoided like the plague by coworkers for fear of retaliation by their employers. Thus, we constantly needed to find new ways of building strength for these workers outside the work context. Perhaps the best example of this strategy was used by the custodial workers' team.

The custodial workers' team that we developed at the Workplace Project was lovingly named L.O.V.E.L.I. (Limpiadores Organizados Venceremos En Long Island—Cleaning Workers United Will Succeed in Long Island) and included several Latino custodial workers, all of whom were members of a large New York service workers' local. Members of this union had been complaining to the Workplace Project for years about the union representatives' lack of responsiveness to their workplace complaints. The old legal clinic would handle these complaints individually, prodding union representatives into listening to their members. In the new model, when one union member came to the Workplace Project complaining of an abusive, discriminatory supervisor and the unresponsiveness of the union, he was encouraged to form a team of his coworkers to address the problem. Together, these workers formed L.O.V.E.L.I. and decided to not simply resolve immediate problems, but to launch a campaign to remove the abusive supervisor and democratize the Long Island district of their union.

La Alianza worked well because it gave us motivation to continue, not to accept what was given to us, but to always forge ahead. La Alianza helped me to continue going forward. They gave me the title leader because I was the first person to seek help for our situation, and I went to inform other people of what was going on. Somehow, there were fellow workers who followed me. We won the transfer of the bad union representative. We also won transfer of the bad supervisor. Most importantly, we were able to get the union to participate more actively with the concerns of the workers. What helped me the most initially was the [intake] workshop, which gave me the notion that we should do something different. From that point, we collected signatures, sent letters to the representatives, the president of the union. We ended up filing a federal lawsuit. All of this pressure led to the reinstatement of Jose Jaimes and Esperanza Velasquez [workers who lost their jobs due to organizing]. This pressure helped us win a new union representative. It was only through our pressure that we won. The Workplace Project helped me, gave me ideas, to bring in more people to meet with us for more strength, to form an organization that we called L.O.V.E.L.I. After having won many successes, we were able to bring in more and more people. (Platero 2002)

L.O.V.E.L.I. fought a yearlong struggle using organizing tactics (meetings, letters, the press, marches, and protests) and a federal lawsuit that resulted in complete success: In the Long Island district of the union, a new business representative was hired and the supervisor was transferred into oblivion. All of the workers who had lost their jobs to this abusive supervisor in retaliation for organizing were reinstated. The campaign was thus a partial victory and a real testament to the power of the team concept. (The legal clinic of old had dealt with complaints about this union for seven years and had never achieved the success L.O.V.E.L.I. achieved in just one year—a union will always respond more quickly to a noisy group of its own members' demands than to those of an outside lawyer.)

### The Small Scope of La Alianza

Admittedly, although the teams we created in La Alianza were useful in creating collective power among workers of the same industry when collective power in the workplace might be difficult or impossible, these teams were small. At their height, the restaurant team had twelve to fifteen members, the custodial workers' team had around twenty, and the factory workers' team had sixty. It was difficult to see how they would actually achieve the objective of building power for Long Island workers given their small size.

Realizing that the teams were small, we focused on finding campaigns that would unify each industry as a concrete way to build power and make real changes in people's lives. The campaigns that were developed out of individual workplace problems of members might make gains for some, but not for the team or the industry. Specific, small-industry campaigns could be fought with allies and might make concrete gains. Thus, though small, L.O.V.E.L.I. succeeded in making these concrete gains because it had a campaign around specific issues and was able to develop a platform of demands on the union and the company, around which they continue to organize. Using this platform, they created a newsletter for custodial workers, and in this way have ultimately reached out to a much wider audience. Most important, Platero notes that the custodial workers saw results on the job.

> The effects of our efforts were that in actuality, at work, they give us more respect. We know more people now, so the employer knows that if something happens at work, there are some people who will help others; they do not want to return to the same situation they faced earlier as a result of our pressure. In this way, the supervisor treats people better than he would had there been no case there. Now, there is much better treatment, there is no more screaming. They ask us to please do whatever needs to be done. There is more respect. (Platero 2002)

Unifying campaigns, fought with worker allies, allowed the team to win power and change for workers in their industry while still being relatively small in size. Nevertheless, the teams' small size and slow growth was always a problem and a major drawback of the program.

## Leadership Skills Development

As mentioned earlier in *The Miner's Canary*, Lani Guinier and Gerald Torres describe the concept of "power-with"—engaging community members in leading their own struggles for justice. As Guinier and Torres describe, community members should lead because only if members lead their own struggle will the struggle continue in the long run. La Alianza was developed on the premise that traditional legal services could not develop true "power-with" among immigrant workers. However, as mentioned, "power-with" is not the easy task of simply putting individuals in leadership positions—it must involve genuine political understanding and analysis by these leaders.

If we were not going to use the legal services model for failure to create genuine immigrant worker leadership, then any new model would have to be evaluated using a more complex definition of leadership. To truly succeed where legal services could not, La Alianza would have to develop the consciousness and capacity of each of these individuals to redefine those positions on their terms, and assess the power of the team in the larger context of their industry and society—thought processes always previously guided by staff organizers. In this section we will examine whether La Alianza's team leaders not only led team meetings, but also if they recruited and engaged new leaders and consistently evaluated the team's progress, taking action to remedy any deficiencies. Finally, we will also evaluate the extent to which the workers' new leadership skills translated into more power in other areas of their lives.

## Leaders Recruit and Engage New Leaders

James MacGregor Burns, in *Leadership*,[10] defines the purpose of leadership as inducing followers to act for certain goals that represent values and motivations of both leaders and followers. The more important form of leadership, then, is transformative leadership, in which one not only recruits new people but engages them with others such that all are raised to higher levels of motivation and morality. Ronald Heifetz, in *Leadership without Easy Answers*, concurs with Burns's definition of transformative leadership, but takes the definition further, adding that leadership is an activity, not a role, that involves organizing people's interests to help them adapt to one another's conflicting values and perspectives. The team members' purposes become fused, so that followers will feel elevated by the relationship and often become more active themselves, thereby creating new cadres of leaders.[11]

Maria Claribel Perez is the leader of the factory workers' team. She first came to the Workplace Project in August 2000 with her sister, complaining of severe sexual harassment and unjust firing at a Long Island factory, and seeking legal services. Over time, the group recognized Perez's consistency, strength, interest, and ability, and deferred increasingly to her leadership. She began to facilitate meetings more often, though she insisted that our previous practice of rotating facilitation continue. Thus, from the outset, it was clear that, as she was doing the work of recruiting more members (as all team members were doing), she was also ensuring that they shared leadership with her. In this way she fulfilled Burns's and Heifitz's definition of transformative leadership. Similarly, Jose Canales Chicas, leader of the restaurant workers' team, defines leaders as those who recruit other leaders.

> A leader is a person who has a good character, a good vocabulary, who has a good personality to treat people well—for example, in order to attract people to be his or her friend (and thereby join the organization). . . . The leader must plan projects, and then get others to believe in the plan and help him carry it out. Simply the fact of being a leader does not mean that things will happen. (Chicas 2001)

But the best example of leadership recruitment by worker leaders was Eduardo Platero, leader of L.O.V.E.L.I. He came to the Workplace Project alone and attended our group intake workshop, where he was told to come back with coworkers. He arrived with five other custodial workers and told us about the abusive workplace. We often used Eduardo as an example of true leadership in organizing—the leader who appeared to be quiet and unassuming but in actuality could organize a group of workers to come to a meeting with greater success than most.

> Leadership is the starting point, it is the beginning of a case. . . . I never thought I was a leader, I simply knew some information that could help the people with their problems. Before L.O.V.E.L.I. I was nothing. I had simply come to the Workplace Project to take a few classes. In the family I made decisions, but at work I was just a normal worker. At the Workplace Project I was just a member who attended various meetings.
>
> I think we (LOVELI) won several successes. I was able to involve lots of other people. I think this is what gave me the title "leader"—having brought in more people to participate. . . . In the group we share ideas, and make plans about how to better the group. But I often represent LOVELI in membership meetings, in the press, in protests and demonstrations. I was really the reason that LOVELI was born. (Platero 2002)

As Heifetz points out, transformative leadership involves more than just recruiting new leaders. As Perez describes, it also includes involving new members and leaders in decision-making and making them feel invested in strategies and their implementation.

I often strategized and thought about M.I.L.I., but I never thought alone, we always did so as a group. We always talked together as a group, thought together as a group, did things together as a group. Simply, as a leader, I had to remind the group of what we had thought earlier, and give information. Being a leader does not mean that I think for everyone, but that we all think for the group. The only important thing about being a leader is to transmit information about what we had thought in the past, but being a leader does not necessarily mean that the leader has to do everything. (Perez 2001)

## Leaders Evaluate Group Progress

In their book *Designing Effective Work Groups*, sociologists Richard Hackman and Richard Walton describe the key leadership functions of effective groups: 1. Diagnosing group deficiencies; 2. taking remedial action to correct deficiencies; 3. forecasting impending environmental changes; 4. preventing deleterious environmental changes or their effects.[12]

The restaurant workers' team had many ups and downs, winning several small campaigns around unpaid wages but never growing beyond twelve or fifteen members. Chicas spent an inordinate amount of time strategizing around member recruitment.

We always have to evaluate or see if our strategies are creating results. If we do not create new results, we have to re-evaluate how we can recruit more people. We were always coming up with new strategies—invite people to a party, invite people to a café to talk with them about the group. We always planned activities in different forms to recruit more people. (Chicas 2001)

These workers' ability to evaluate their teams' progress was never in doubt; what is remarkable is the fact that they all diagnosed group deficiencies and took remedial action to correct deficiencies on their own, without prompting by organizers or attorneys. Such evaluative functions are almost always carried out by staff organizers, but in the team model the new leaders felt great responsibility for their success. In part, this was due to the fact that each team did not have its own staff organizer; one attorney/organizer worked with all three, and so the team leaders knew that they were the only ones thinking exclusively about their team's success. In fact, Perez states that some of her most important functions as a leader were evaluative.

I always evaluated the welfare of the group—as a leader I always had to think about ways to keep people from leaving the group, what the group could do to solve its members' problems. Now we meet with other groups sometimes to see what is going on with them. The group is always considering for itself new strategies. (Perez 2001)

## Transferable Leadership Skills

Interviews with these three leaders indicate that the leadership skills they gained through La Alianza changed their lives. First, at a minimal level, all of the leaders became more involved in other Workplace Project activities. Perez explains how getting involved as a leader in La Alianza led to other leadership roles at the Workplace Project, in large part because she felt more self-confidence in her ability to lead.

Transforming from a worker to a leader is very important because I learned many things, that as workers we can have our rights and our opportunities in this country. And also, I am not only the leader of the factory workers group, but am also now the vice-president of the women's cooperative—UNITY Housecleaners—and a member of the board of directors as well. . . . In the beginning one feels that one does not have the capacity to do such things, but little by little I began to have more confidence, experiencing so much, receiving so much guidance, and seeing the experience of other people. In addition, at the same time we were receiving leadership training seminars. So that is where one learns a little more, and one will say, "I could do this as well." When I was not a leader, I did not have this same way of thinking. Now, I have to be in front, I have to present the agenda and all that. After becoming a leader, one realizes that it involves more commitment, and one must be more serious about it, and think about what one is doing. It is a big responsibility. I became a leader, and had to be very involved in the end, whereas in the beginning I thought, "No, what am I doing here, I can't do this." (Perez 2001)

Chicas also states that his experiences with La Alianza have made him feel more self-confident about his leadership abilities.

I was not a leader before coming to the Workplace Project. I was not, I did not have the capacity, I did not even have the dream of being a leader. I was not trained. Now, I feel more at liberty to express myself, I feel like I have more capacity and training. When I spoke [in front of the group] for the first time, I trembled in my pants. This was the first time I had to lead a V.E.R. [Venceremos Empleados de Restaurantes—Restaurant Workers Will Succeed, the Restaurant Workers' Team] meeting and write up the agenda. Now that I am a leader, I would help others—we have to let other people know their rights, what they are due. If a person does not give, he cannot receive. (Chicas, 2001)

Perez seems to be most excited about using her new self-confidence to help other workers. She describes how her work situation has changed.

I believe that, there in the factory where I am now—I believe that not only coming to the Workplace Project, but also becoming a leader, has been something good for me. Although I was a little scared at first, afterwards I felt good, because all the women in my factory, some said to me, "We have a leader, a star here, because she is going to help us." This was because everyone saw me when we came out on Channel 41, and nobody could believe it. They said, "When you speak, when you explain things, with the way you express things it seems as if you have no fear of anything, and that you are very sure of what you are doing."

Learning so many things, being a part of the Alliance for Justice, has helped me a lot, not only to defend myself, but also to be able to defend other people. I can say with more confidence, "There is a place where they can help you, where they can advise you. I learned a lot in this place and now I am helping and advising people myself." . . . Some people will always have fear. But when I passed the information to everyone, everyone knew, and something good is that after passing out the information the bosses have a little more fear of me, they know that I am not alone, they know that I already know many things that perhaps I did not know before. They know I can use the information not only for myself but also to transmit it to others in the factory. This is very important. The foreman always has a little fear of me now. (Perez, 2001)

Chicas describes a similar experience in the workplace.

In my work, before I was afraid to speak to my boss. Now as a leader, I no longer have fear to speak. I used to clean a stove where I had to use chemicals, and I never spoke up about it. Now I can defend myself. (Chicas 2001)

For Perez, these new abilities have also transformed how her family views her.

I have changed. Sometimes in the family—they never see me standing and speaking in the front [of the room], that one could be leading a group, or do all the things that I never did before. For example, one time my mother came to the Workplace Project, and it was my turn to lead, she said to me, "Clari, I had no idea you could do that." It is something that the family has never seen me do, and when they see it they do not believe it. Since they do not have a lot of knowledge about what I am doing, they do not know whether to support me or not. But I continue to explain things to them, and they continue to learn. They have come to support us in various protests. Now yes—before they did not even understand what organizing was. My brother likes what I am doing very much, but his wife does not allow him to participate for religious reasons. In some ways it is good that they see me differently, because if they think they need some help with something at work, they believe I can help them. (Perez 2001)

For all of the leaders, a consistent theme is their excitement over being able to use their new skills and abilities to help other workers. Perez names this new spirit *compañerismo*—the spirit of working collectively—and attributes it to her experience with the team. Platero exudes a similar enthusiasm over his new abilities.

Now, when I encounter a worker who is being abused, I know what to say, what to recommend to them. I have knowledge, I know never to stay with my arms crossed, doing nothing. It is very important to have this knowledge. I can use these skills, making other people know their rights that they have as workers, informing them that if their boss comes to scream at them or fire them without justification, this is exploitation, and cannot occur without a good justification. In part, it is because of fear that a lot of people do not wish to organize. We teach them not to be afraid, that they should confront their problems, and organize, and invite more co-workers. I no longer have fear of speaking up, or seeking whatever help I need. . . . I have stayed with the group because it is somewhat of a calling, to make sure my co-workers know that there are laws and rights, so that the worker knows that he can defend himself on the job. (Platero 2002)

Nevertheless, despite the fact that these leaders are most anxious to discuss how their new skills can be used to help their fellow workers, they do also indicate that their new abilities have changed their lives personally as well. Both Perez and Chicas indicate that their experiences with their teams inspired them to increase their skills and abilities in other aspects of their life.

> It sparked in me the consciousness to want to better myself. I believe that before I did not think as I think now, before coming to the Workplace Project. For example, I had not thought about wanting to better myself, or wanting to learn English, wanting to study more. It gave me the idea that with more study I would not necessarily have to work in a factory, I could work for the government, or any dignified job. Now I know I have the capacity to do so. (Perez 2001)
>
> Once I became involved at the Workplace Project, I also decided to go to school. I can also do more within the Workplace Project itself. One day at the Workplace Project I was asked to type up a list of names, and this inspired me to want to go to school to learn English. (Chicas 2001)

Most important, these new leadership skills seem to have achieved exactly what was missing in the old legal clinic model—workers' confidence that they can solve their own problems through collective power, without depending on lawyers, as Perez so eloquently states.

> Since coming to the Workplace Project my life has changed completely. Because I no longer think that I cannot do something, I always think that I have the capacity to do it. I have the capacity to demonstrate that yes, as workers we can do many important things. (Perez 2001)

## Conclusion

La Alianza was not the creation of one person, or even four people, but the work and thought of many workers and staff members over a period of a year and a half, during which time the model was constantly tweaked and improved. One of the key reasons for its success was its ever-changing nature; it adapted to the needs of different situations at different points in time. For example, while we had originally envisioned that all of the teams would comprise workers of the same industry but different workplaces, L.O.V.E.L.I. ended up being formed around workers not only from the same workplace, but also the same union local. Realizing the need for flexibility, we in no way seek to promote La Alianza as a model for wide-scale replication; we only hope that our experiences are useful to other practitioners seeking to empower immigrant workers or considering new models of law and organizing.

Of course, certain aspects of the model are easily replicable. First, La Alianza provides evidence that every step of the process an immigrant worker—or any underprivileged person—undergoes to resolve a problem can occur in a group context. In other words, intake can occur in a group orientation, problem-solving for individuals can occur in a group strategizing session, and every step of strategy implementation can occur as a group, from writing letters to power brokers to visiting them directly. The advantages of group work are that it is quickly demonstrated to workers that acting as a collective is more effective than any individual effort, and that they are capable of doing so without a lawyer.

Most important, by forming their own groups, workers can develop leadership skills that are transferable to all aspects of their lives. Indeed, the testimonies of Chicas, Perez, and Platero about the ways in which their newfound leadership skills have affected their lives beyond work call for a new definition of leadership. Clearly, members of any worker organizing effort are not just workers—they are complex human beings who must confront several different points of power besides their employers. Thus, genuine leadership by immigrant workers means developing skills that can be used to change the balance of power in these many different contexts. In this way, immigrant workers can win increased power and control over their own lives.

## Notes

1. Lani Guinier and Gerald Torres, *The Miner's Canary* (Harvard University Press, Cambridge, MA, 2002).

2. Though untraditional, out of respect for their wisdom and experience, the perspectives of the workers quoted in this article will be treated with equal validity as those of academics.

3. The Workplace Project is a Latino immigrant worker organizing center based in Hemptsead, Long Island. Its mission is to organize Latino immigrant workers to fight exploitation in the workplace. Saru Jayaraman worked there as a legal extern in the fall of 1999, and as the attorney/organizer in charge of the new law and organizing program in 2000 and 2001. Jose Canales Chicas, Maria Claribel Perez, and Eduardo Platero were all member-leaders of the industry-based teams created through this new program.

4. Richard Marisco, "Working for Social Change and Preserving Client Autonomy: Is There a Role for 'Facilitative' Lawyering?" *Clinical Law Review*, vol. 1, spring 1995, p. 639.

5. Ibid.

6. William P. Quigley, "Reflections of Community Organizers: Lawyering for Empowerment of Community Organizations," *Ohio Northern University Law Review*, vol. 21, 1994, p. 455.

7. Anthony V. Alfieri, "Book Review: Practicing Community," *Harvard Law Review*, vol. 107, May 1994, p. 1747.

8. Gerald Lopez, *Rebellious Lawyering* (Westview Press, Boulder, 1992), p. 49.

9. In discussing the creation and growth of La Alianza, "we" refers to Saru Jayaraman, Jose Canales Chicas, Maria Claribel Perez, Eduardo Platero, and several other worker leaders who contributed much to the model's development over time.

10. James MacGregor Burns, *Leadership* (Harper & Row, 1981), pp. 9–28.

11. Ronald A. Heifetz, *Leadership without Easy Answers* (Harvard University Press, 1994), pp. 13–27.

12. Richard J. Hackman, Richard Walton, et al. *Designing Effective Work Groups* (Jossey-Bass, 1986), pp. 72–119.

## 7

AI-JEN POO AND ERIC TANG

# Center Stage: Domestic Workers Organizing in the Global City

The dawn of the twenty-first century poses many new questions for a renewed feminist movement, and indeed for a renewed popular left in general. But perhaps some of these questions are not so new. To be sure, we struggle with staying faithful to living an activism that takes into consideration race, gender, class, and sexuality. And while the past twenty years may have taught us to adequately recite this mantra, our practical commitment to it in the form of organizing, activism, and the culture of the movement leaves something to be desired. More specifically, we are speaking of the ways in which the revitalized labor movement and the civil rights/antiracist and contemporary feminist interventions have each found their own particular way of marginalizing those who reside at their common intersection: women of color, particularly those who migrate from the Third World. These women are somehow always and already outside the parameters of these "centers of struggle." This may sound like an old and familiar critique. Indeed, it may seem as if we have beat to death the topic of margin-center relationship. "Moving on" and "rebuilding" a damaged and fragmented left has been the order of the day for some time.

Yet, simultaneously, there are new players who have introduced themselves to this seemingly old issue. The rapid globalization of labor over the past thirty years—from the Malaysian microchip worker of the "free trade zones" to migrant Filipina and West Indian domestic workers in the global corporate city, to the African American woman compelled to take up flexible, temporary, and invisible labor in the punitive "workfare" state—demonstrates the ways in which the work and movement of women of color around the world are a generative force in global corporate hegemony.[1] So, if the popular left has grown tired of being reminded of how race, gender, and sexuality intersect, if it is weary of devising ways to break down the distance between the center and the periphery, then they've missed an essential shift in the global economy. Working women of color worldwide are already at center stage. Global capitalism claims—in no uncertain terms—that the periphery is in the core.

Third World women who work as domestics play a central role in New York City's restructured economy. Domestic workers provide a number of services for the city's global corporate elite: They are house-keepers, child caregivers, elderly companions, private tutors, and per-sonal assistants, to name but a few of their most general roles. As with many other migrant Third World laborers in the global city, domestic workers are a backbone for the booming wealth of the new First World economy. Their central role as producers is facilitated by a combina-tion of punitive legislative action (ranging from anti-immigration acts to labor laws that explicitly exclude domestic workers), "free trade" agreements between the United States and Third World nations that seek to "capture" low-wage labor from the Third World, and the aban-donment of a social welfare state in American cities.[2] The women workers who make up the domestic industry in New York City have migrated primarily from the Philippines, the West Indies, Jamaica, Trinidad, Guyana, St. Vincent, St. Lucia, and Barbados. They are part of the new working class in the global corporate city. Yet despite their central (and invisible) position at the site of production, they have yet to be picked up by the formal labor movement's radar; for that matter, broader social justice movements as a whole have failed to include these women workers in their agendas as well. Nevertheless, they have not been dissuaded from organizing.

The organizing efforts of Filipina domestic workers in New York City who are part of the Women Workers Project of CAAAV: Orga-nizing Asian Communities,[3] and the immigrant women in the city-wide workers' campaign known as Domestic Workers United (DWU) are examples of this. Their passage to the United States along the circuits of global capital and their "disenfranchisement"—through legislative and judicial acts of anti-immigration and citizenship ex-clusion, and through traditional modes of political organizing that fail to redefine meanings of work in the new era—illuminate the par-ticular challenges of this otherwise invisible labor force. The ways in which domestic workers are organizing challenge these multiple exclusions by creating alternative worker communities for Third World women. These spaces are much more than autonomous sites for political organizing. Rather, they are spaces where women script alternative forms of citizenship and political participation—forms that we all must learn to adopt under a global capitalist era and that are way ahead of the left when it comes to recognizing new formations of identity politics.

## Forced Migration

In New York City, poor Asian immigrant women have essentially one option in the labor market: the sweatshop. The New York City sweatshop takes on many forms: garment factory, restaurant, nail salon, laundry, and the home. All these workplaces share certain characteristics: no regulation, harsh surveillance, low wages, long hours, and threats of physical and sexual violence. Conditions in these sweatshops are linked to those faced by women laboring in the Free Trade Zones[4] (FTZs) of the Third World. In fact, the opening of such FTZs in Asia, Latin America, and the Caribbean has led to the internal economic, cultural, and social ruptures that compel many Third World women to leave their homelands in the first place.[5] In the Philippines, the legacy of United States militarized imperialism continues to structure its economic development. Ironically, the Philippines is often referred to as an economic "miracle," when in fact it is miraculous for its model of rapid (uneven) development that has led to mass poverty, environmental degradation, unemployment, the deterioration of social welfare programs, and mass migration—particularly among women—from rural to urban areas, from agricultural production to services for business-class tourists and FTZ production (production of a range of products made for United States companies that include such items as computer hardware in Malaysia and garments made in every Southeast Asian nation). We are talking about the near-complete control that American companies have in these zones, ranging from the right to union-bust to the right to determine environmental standards (or lack thereof) to the right to violate local laws. These are rights granted by the FTZs.

FTZ workers labor where governments overlook violations and slavelike conditions, where organizing is criminalized, and where working conditions are deadly. Many women are compelled to then migrate from Asia in search of alternatives to FTZ labor; and American immigration and foreign policy then provide the conduits for workers to move into sweatshop industries within the United States. Thus, most Third World workers in search of low-wage jobs in the United States don't leave their homelands as a matter of choice. As scholar/activist Grace Chang notes in her book *Disposable Domestics*, United States–controlled free trade agreements that place Third World nations in debt and compel them to open themselves to lawless FTZs and their accompanying violence also serve the purpose of compelling and "capturing" low-wage labor from the Third World, particularly the labor of women workers.[6]

Once in the United States, Asian and other Third World women became the ground level upon which New York City's economic boom of 1990s was built. This is more than mere metaphor; for along the ground floors and in the basements of the immaculate buildings lining the Upper East and West Sides of Manhattan, "servant quarters"—a line of cell-like rooms—house women from Latin America, the Caribbean, and the Philippines. These women clean and care for the children of the wealthy families who live above. Domestic workers extend the wealth of the global city not only through their labor output in the homes of the city's elite, but also through the many new service economies that their employers consume on the disposable time and income made available through highly exploitable domestic service. Indeed, domestic workers are integral to business-class consumption of new luxuries such as grocery delivery services, exclusive gyms, gourmet markets and restaurants, extravagant beauty salons and spas, and vacationing. In addition to cleaning and providing security and child care, domestic workers shop, wait for deliveries, drop off and pick up dry cleaning, and escort children to gym classes. They feed and bathe children as parents go to fitness centers, enjoy the opera, get their nails done, and travel abroad. Domestic workers are, in effect, the "key link" in a highly integrated service economy for the city's wealthy class. And yet, despite this central role, and despite being the caregiver to the most important elements of their employers' lives—families and property—domestic workers are still often paid less per week than their employers spend on a new pair of shoes.

Jennifer, a Filipina nanny working in the Upper West Side and a member of the Women Workers Project, describes the contradictions:

The children I take care of have special classes three of the five days per week. It's either ballet, or piano, or martial arts, or painting. I have to pick them up from school, drop the older one off at one class, and take the younger one to the ballet for toddlers, come back around to get the dry cleaning, and then come home to a message that my boss will be one hour late because she went to get her nails done. One and a half hours later, she returns. And she has forgotten to prepare my salary and wonders if I could wait until Monday to get paid. If I could afford to be without work for even a week, I would leave this job. I have to send money home.

## A Global Labor Force

The roots of this deep exploitation, invisibility, and flexibility of contemporary domestic work finds its roots in the racial and gender legacies of American labor—a legacy that can be traced (at least) as far back as slavery and the antebellum period. Since the abolition of institutionalized slavery, black women have worked as domestics. The overwhelming presence of black women in the industry at the turn of the century, combined with the eventual influx of Irish immigrant women domestics, drove many native-born white women to leave the industry. Before long, Irish immigrant women also sought to distance themselves from paid domestic work as it increasingly became characterized as definitively "black women's work." Like earlier European immigrant workers, Irish domestic workers understood that their transition into whiteness would be impossible if they did not disidentify with the paid domestic workers industry.[7] Thus, during the height of industrialization, Irish and other white working-class women sought wage labor in the garment and textile factories. They chose the factory sweatshop over the domestic sweatshop. And, as more options for wage labor outside the home emerged for women over the course of the twentieth century, many of these positions excluded women of color. As a result, the domestic industry has remained overwhelmingly dominated by black and eventually Asian and Latina women workers.

The unambiguous color and gender of domestic work in the United States is the primary justification for a long history of punitive legislation, negligence, and the criminalization of the industry. Today the industry remains as unregulated and as dangerously exploitative as ever before. Indeed, if the industry has undergone changes, it has not been in the area of workers' rights, power, and dignity, but in the form of a demographic shift in the workforce. The black civil rights revolution of the 1960s opened up new opportunities for some African American women. Although the majority of African American women are still restricted to low-wage labor and in some cases remain in the domestic sector, a large number were tracked and networked into industries in which there is some unionization or state regulation, such as home health care and institutionalized child care. In addition, the civil rights revolution opened up possibilities for many black women in the civil sector.

In the early twenty-first century, immigrants from the Third World now dominate the domestic work industry. And much like their early turn-of-the-century counterparts, they are viewed as nonworkers/noncitizens; they are routinely punished through legislation; and they have been abandoned by the formal labor movement. In an effort to compel, confine, and punish this labor force, a new set of social control policies and practices has been enacted. The social control measures draw particular strength from the anti-immigrant consensus that dominates contemporary American politics and culture. The all-out assault on immigrant rights—from the federal Immigration Reform Act of 1997 to the particularly heinous California initiative known as Proposition 187—has emboldened employers of domestic workers to use the threat of deportation and detention as a means of exerting full control over the industry. If workers dare fight for higher wages, better conditions, and more reasonable hours, they run the risk of activating numerous agencies hell-bent on imprisoning and deporting undocumented immigrant workers. Moreover, many employers extend this coercive activity beyond wages, working conditions, and hours. Indeed, it is also used to facilitate sexual harassment, psychological abuse, and isolation.

Physical isolation is perhaps the most effective and damaging form of control that many migrant domestics face. Unlike African American domestics of the early to mid-twentieth century, today's Third World migrant is a truly transnational worker with few ties to her ethnic community in the U.S. city. She is often sent from her homeland directly to the employer's residence and is completely isolated from the ethnic enclave. The employer holds her passport, visa, access to cash, and in many cases controls the degree of contact the worker has with the outside world. Carol H. DeLeon, director of the Women Workers Project of CAAAV and a former domestic worker, recalls how her first employers used the tactic of isolation:

I was isolated for a long period of time. I finally contacted a friend who came before me from Hong Kong. She came to visit me in the suburbs and showed me where the train station was, and how to get to Queens. So the following weekend, I bought my ticket to New York City, and I met my friend at Grand Central Station. We got on the #7 Train to Queens and I searched for my [Filipina] community. When I returned, my boss was shocked to find that I went to Queens. She told me never to go there again because "It's a very dangerous place. If anything happens to you, I'll be responsible." This was the same woman who had me freezing to death because she wouldn't provide me with a winter coat.

Carol had left the Philippines at the age of twenty-three to work as a domestic in Hong Kong before deciding to move to the United States with an American family that was moving back to New York. At first glance, Carol's travels suggest a certain "freedom" of mobility that few workers seem to have. Yet her travels were part of a highly restricted set of immigration labor policies aimed at controlling and confining workers as they move along the circuits of global capital.

**The Politics of Visas**

The vast majority of domestics in New York City are undocumented. Employers use the promise of sponsorship to keep workers in abusive conditions for years, while an even more common threat is incarceration or deportation. Most workers have endured numerous hardships in order to work in the U.S. and be able to send some money home. The thought of getting put into an Immigration and Naturalization Service (INS) detention center or being deported home empty-handed or in debt is enough of a threat to silence most workers. Immigration laws provide employers with a constant pool of domestic labor to exploit without recourse.

Migrant domestics from Asia come to the United States on a number of different employment-based visas including B1, A3, and G5 visas. Every year over two hundred thousand B1s are issued for temporary noncitizen workers and United States citizens based in foreign countries. In the United States, B1 visa holders are mostly either corporate executives here to work temporarily or their "bound" domestic workers. "Bound" here has three primary meanings: First, women are bound to the global economy as their labor is captured through a combination of global corporate policies in the homeland and migrant labor needs in the "receiving" countries of the West; second, they are bound by immigration laws in the U.S. that allow employers to fully control not only labor conditions, but social and familial conditions for the women workers—the employers hold on to passports, visas, and work papers, all with the backing of the INS; third, "bound" here refers to the ways in which women workers are forced to take up low-wage labor because of their race, gender, and undocumented status.

Regardless of employment conditions, as soon as a B1 visa–holding domestic worker leaves her employer, she becomes undocumented—a situation that leads to widespread exploitation. One of the first campaign cases taken up by CAAAV's Women Workers' Project involved a domestic worker on a B1 visa from Hong Kong who was made to work seven days per week, seventeen hours per day, by an executive of Credit Lyonnais Securities Asia, an international financial institution. CAAAV's Women Workers Project was one of the first organizing efforts to target and provide media exposure about the corporations whose B1 visa–holding employees bring abuse to their domestics. The worker involved in that case, Maria, is now an organizer with the Women Workers Project, helping to organize advocacy campaigns for other exploited domestic workers. She often tells other workers, "I was afraid in the beginning because I had no friends or family here, but I had to get my dignity back. When you are in that position, you will find support."

A3 and G5 visa holders are domestics who work for employees of the World Bank, IMF, or other foreign governments. A3 and G5 visas also bind workers to their employers. In addition, these employers hold diplomatic immunity, making it nearly impossible for workers to seek justice against abusive employers. Andolan Organizing South Asian Workers, a South Asian domestic workers organization based in Jackson Heights, Queens, has organized several successful campaigns targeting abusive diplomat employers in New York City. The Campaign for Migrant Domestic Workers Rights in Washington, D.C., has also documented a general pattern of abuse where domestic workers work under slaverylike conditions for their diplomat employers.

One G5 worker, "Vivian," found Domestic Workers United while looking for a way out of an exploitative situation. Her diplomat employer did not pay her for nine months of work, and she asked to return home. Her employer then began paying her $250 per month, so that she could buy her own plane ticket back to Africa. Of her experience, she says, "If I had known what the conditions would be, I never would have come. I only wanted to go to school. He thought I would never leave because of the visa, but I did. Slavery is over."

However, the abuse is not only within these visa categories. Rather, they reflect the overall nature of immigration policies and practices in the United States that have created a climate of pervasive fear among immigrant workers. These conditions have created de facto immunity for all employers of domestics and undocumented workers generally.

## No Legal Protections

Those who seek solutions to the widespread abuses of domestics brought on by immigration laws have found that local and national employment and labor laws do not provide any recourse. Not only do labor enforcement agencies turn a blind eye to abuses in the domestic work industry, many laws that serve to protect workers' rights specifically exclude domestic workers. A hard-won victory of the labor movement, the National Labor Relations Act (NLRA) was passed as part of the New Deal in the early part of the twentieth century. This act gave workers the right to organize and bargain collectively for better working conditions. It also protected workers from retaliation from their employers for organizing. The only two groups of workers excluded from this act and the protections it provided were domestic workers and farm workers. It comes as no surprise that these were two industries dominated by workers of color at the time. Farm work was largely done by African American, Chicano, Filipino, and Chinese workers. Domestic work was done largely by Native Americans, African Americans, and Chicanas. These were also industries in which working conditions resembled institutionalized slavery the most. Today the NLRA continues to exclude farm workers and domestics. Finally, most laws that protect workers from discrimination only regulate workplaces that have fifteen workers or more. These exclusions reflect a system that explicitly disregards and renders invisible what is regarded as "women's labor."

This is not to say that there haven't been any efforts at reforming the domestic work industry over the past century. African American labor leaders who were connected with the early "building years" of the democratic union movement sought to extend union activity to black women domestics in New York City. These organizing efforts were short-lived, however, as larger and more powerful unions refused to legitimize domestic work.

Interestingly, the early twentieth century also witnessed several industry reform initiatives on the part of employers—particularly white, middle-class women. From 1933 to 1940, reformers in various states called for legislation that would establish minimum standards for the domestic work industry. Later, reformers fought for domestic workers to be included in the National Labor Relations Act. All of these reform efforts were led by white elite and middle-class employers who believed that a stable pool of paid domestic labor would keep white working-class women working in the domestic sphere, diverting them from the industrial jobs in textile and garment factories. In the early twentieth century, some privileged white women also saw the employment of a domestic as a status symbol, a means of elevating their own status from housewife to household manager. In this sense, the formalization of paid domestic work would serve as a means to formalize their positioning as a managerial class.

## Alternative Citizenship

The Women Workers Project of CAAAV seeks justice, dignity, and self-determination for domestic workers across the entire city. Toward this end, they, along with Andolan Organizing South Asian Workers, have helped to create Domestic Workers United (DWU), a New York City–wide multiracial movement of domestic workers. The main campaign of DWU is the fight for a standard contract. In 1999 the Women Workers Project helped draft a model contract and a series of guidelines for employers; DWU was the vehicle that pressured employers to use the contract. Members conducted regular outreach to workers throughout Manhattan and Brooklyn, and organized monthly meetings to strategize the campaign. Workers who participated in this process identified three main goals: 1) gaining respect and recognition for domestic workers; 2) getting an industry-wide standard; and 3) reaching multiracial unity among workers. A multiracial steering committee of domestic workers was constituted to provide leadership for the campaign, and within three months of DWU's formation, a general membership base of over 150 members had been developed. In addition to working on the contract campaign, members are also developing training curricula, conducting surveys of their peers on working conditions, and researching both contract enforcement strategies and state-level legislation to achieve policy reform.[8] Since the summer of 2001, members have been organizing for passage of a city council bill and resolution to help protect the rights of domestic workers in New York City. The bill regulates employment agencies that place domestic workers, which are notorious for charging illegal fees and sending workers into subminimum-wage jobs. The new law compels employment agencies to provide employers with a code of conduct, including both employers' legal obligations and a suggested standard for the conditions of employment, such as paid holidays and sick days, and notice of termination. The bill also requires a written statement of working conditions for every placement. The council resolution calls for respect and dignity for domestic workers and urges all domestic employers to use the Domestic Workers United standard contract. In addition, the resolution declares establishment of an annual "Domestic Workers Recognition Day." After months of meetings with city council members, the introduction of the bill and resolution was announced on March 24, 2002, by a multiracial group of about forty domestic workers on the steps of city hall. The legislation, while limited, is a new foothold for workers in this movement who desire to continue building their power.

The struggle of Asian and other Third World migrant domestic workers described here brings to light a cultural and economic politics that is violently oppressive and seemingly omnipotent in its global reach. Race, class, gender, and nation exploitation are the modes through which it carries forward its agenda; indeed, today's new global labor force is developed and set forth by the creation and re-creation of racist and gendered logics that function as the backbone of an economic system that has been global since its very inception. Here then, "restructuring" refers not only to the bare and destructive economic policies orchestrated by the World Bank and the International Monetary Fund; it also names the restructuring of racial, gendered, and national oppression during a contradictory era that requires the liquidation of national borders on the one hand (in the form of First World nations that are fundamentally reliant on the wealth produced by Third World migrant labor *within* its borders) and a growing reactionary cultural nationalism on the other (epitomized by anti-immigrant U.S. policies such as the Immigrant Reform and Personal Responsibility Acts of 1996 and the draconian California state initiative known as Proposition 187). Maintaining this contradiction requires a new—but hardly sophisticated—set of cultural and economic politics that can provide a rationale for a moment in history that is illogical to its very core. For instance, it is precisely this restructured racial, gendered, and national politics that has allowed the Filipino government to use the phrase "modern-day heroes" to describe the millions of Filipinas who pay off the nation's insurmountable debt by working as indentured servants throughout the world.

Among the many tasks for today's social justice movement in the United States is the need to develop new organizing strategies, a new political language and culture, and coalition politics that can effectively expose the fault lines of contemporary global capitalism and build resistance at the sites wherein these fault lines are most deeply experienced. These sites include not only domestic workers among Third World migrant women, but the many other workers who subsist in the temporary, domestic, and flexible global economy: the workfare worker, the prison laborer, the garment sweatshop worker, the pieceworkers whose living rooms have become floor shops for major garment and technology corporations—to name but a few. Yet as the various sectors of the social justice movement, particularly the core labor movement, experience a self-proclaimed rebirth, it is apparent that these particular laboring bodies are far removed from the center of the new resistance movement. Save for a few notable examples, undocumented migrant laborers are at best a marginal voice in the renewed and supposedly immigrant-friendly union movement. While labor has recently given some lip service to legalizing the status of undocumented workers, it has yet to take a firm stand against their neoliberal allies who have facilitated the passage of some of the worst anti-immigrant policies in modern American history. At best, the renewed labor movement seeks a judicial granting of citizenship to immigrants who have proved themselves good producers and earners for the United States economy. Such a view ignores the fact that the very presence of undocumented and super-exploited migrant workers in the United States is a direct consequence of a Third World economy that has been deeply ruptured by the United States and its First World counterparts. Such violence has occurred in the name of American citizenship: the right to consume inexhaustibly, the right to unmitigated competition; the right to own (both property and labor) without interference; the right to privatize for the public good. The labor movement, with its continual talk of living wages (in the public sphere) for working (read nuclear) families, upright citizens, and decent folk who believe in the promise of the American dream have yet to challenge what is fundamentally oppressive to the undocumented migrant worker: American citizenship itself.

For the domestic workers who organize within CAAAV and as part of the city-wide movement being led by Domestic Workers United, the task is not only to fight for dignity, workplace rights, and appropriate monetary compensation, but also to bring forth an *alternative citizenship*. What is at stake for the women of this movement is an opportunity to challenge the citizenship of consumerism, ownership, privatization, and exploitation that structures this global movement, and that has led to the further destruction of their homelands. Political organizing is how this alternative citizenship comes to fruition. Ideologically, spaces such as Domestic Workers United recognize these women as transnational laborers who are not confined to the boundaries of the nation-state. Practically, DWU seeks a holistic view to the fundamental value of labor. These women are the counterforce to patriarchal nationalisms within their communities; they are caregivers who earn the family wage; and they build multiracial struggle through their parallel histories. Strategically, movements like DWU teach the broader social justice movement that the heretofore domestic laborers like manual laborers deserve to be recognized as workers in the public sphere. To be sure, "Third World women" can no longer stand as a particularized category within the feminist movement because, under globalization, these women have been integrated into every circuit of the race/gender nexus. We cannot imagine a space in which they fail to be integral.

## Notes

1. For a discussion on temporary, flexible, and domestic work, see Chandra Mohanty's introduction to M. Jacqui Alexander and Chandra Mohanty, eds., *Feminist Genealogies, Colonial Legacies, Democratic Futures* (New York: Routledge, 1996).

2. See Grace Chang, *Disposable Domestics: Immigrant Women Workers in the Global Economy* (Boston: South End Press, 2000).

3. CAAAV, once Committee against Anti-Asian Violence, has formally changed its name to CAAAV: Organizing Asian Communities to reflect its move away from class-blind "hate crime" advocacy and emphasize our focus on low-income community organizing and low-wage/no-wage worker organizing.

4. Free Trade Zones are areas set aside by a government or state (country) for the manufacture and export of goods by companies that are, for the most part, owned outside of the state. Tax incentives, cheap rent, and free utilities encourage foreign investment and the installation of companies. Because they tend to be in countries that have very high unemployment rates, they have access to a very large pool of cheap labor. Laborers in many places are mostly women, who are forced to work

long hours for little pay, endure sexual harassment and abuse, and endure environmental hazards without access to any means of changing their situations.

5. For a good discussion on forced migration, see Saskia Sassen, *The Mobility of Capital and Labor* (Cambridge: Cambridge University Press, 1990).

6. Chang, *Disposable Domestics*, 1–17.

7. As Matthew Frye Jacobson points out in *Whiteness of a Different Color: European Immigrants and the Alchemy of Race*, race in America has always been an unstable category in immigrants from Poland, Ireland, and other places, moving from racially "other" to whiteness over time.

8. See "Dignity and the Domestic Sweatshop," *CAAAV Voice*, vol. 10, no. 4, fall 2000, pp. 4–7.

MONIKA BATRA

# Organizing in the South Asian Domestic Worker Community: Pushing the Boundaries of the Law and Organizing Project

Lawyers in the law and organizing community recognize that what makes their project successful is the presence of community organizing efforts by the community organizations with whom these lawyers collaborate. However, it is not enough for these lawyers to recognize the importance of the role of organizing in the struggle for social change[1]; these lawyers must take the time to learn about the history and nature of organizing within the particular community with whom they seek to collaborate as lawyers. Only then will these lawyers be able to help craft particular legal strategies in ways that will strengthen organizing efforts rather than weaken them. This chapter argues that given the particular difficulties of organizing within the South Asian domestic worker community, lawyers who seek to work with this community must be aware of the nature and history of organizing within this community. Only then will these lawyers be able to avoid hindering the growth of organizations that are struggling to organize such a community; only then will they be able to successfully support, maintain, and facilitate the development of these organizations.[2]

This chapter is grounded in my experiences as a core organizer of Workers' Awaaz. Workers' Awaaz is the first organization in the U.S. committed to organizing South Asian domestic workers.[3] Part 1 will provide a history of the law and organizing project. Part 2 will argue that the implementation of such a project will help lawyers avoid the common traps of traditional lawyering. Part 3 will discuss the nature of domestic work in the South Asian context and show its conflicts with traditional organizing strategies. Part 5 will discuss concrete ways in which lawyers in the law and organizing project can use their knowledge of the nature and history of organizing South Asian domestic workers to support the development of such organizing efforts. The conclusion calls for lawyers in the law and organizing project to be aware of the nature and history of organizing within the communities with whom they seek to collaborate as lawyers.

## The Law and Organizing Project: Putting Community Organizing at the Center

In their article *A Critical Reflection on Law and Organizing*, Scott Cummings and Ingrid Eagly provide a useful historical account of the evolution of the "law and organizing project."[4] They trace the law and organizing movement in part to 1) the progressive critique of the law generally,[5] and litigation specifically, as a social change vehicle; and 2) the postmodern critique of lawyers as social change agents. They point out that these two critiques of litigation and lawyers led to an increased emphasis on the primacy of mass mobilization and popular protest as the basis for political and economic change and an increased skepticism toward the inability of litigation to produce meaningful reform.

### The Progressive Critique of the Role of Litigation

The predominant critique of cause lawyers is that they are heavily inclined toward litigation as the preferred means to achieve reform goals.[6] As a result, cause lawyers overwhelm movements with this single-minded commitment to litigation as a tool for social change.[7] Litigation often serves to atomize struggles, dividing and separating rather than uniting those who desire social change.[8] Moreover, the limited ideological biases of legal professionals, which privilege individual controversies to the detriment of collective struggles and goals, unconsciously narrow lawyers' conceptions of movement ends.[9] Litigation effectively silences poor people by requiring the repackaging of client grievances in a form the court can understand.[10] In the context of community organizations, litigation undermines organizing efforts by reinforcing reliance on lawyers and co-opting potential community leaders by paying them off with a settlement or judgment award.[11] In sum, with their unfettered and unchallenged use of litigation, traditional cause lawyers push social movements in narrow directions that are at best ineffective and at worst harmful.[12] And in so doing, they tend to reaffirm more than resist and challenge status quo hierarchies.

### The Postmodern Critique of Lawyers

The postmodern critique of lawyers urges lawyers first to recognize their power, and then to share it, in order to both foster client empowerment and create meaningful community change strategies.[13] George Lopez argues that a "rebellious" practice must create a collaboration between lawyer and client that draws on both of their experiences and lawyering skills in order to alleviate the client's subordinated position in society.[14] Lopez asserts that both lawyers and laypeople possess "lawyering" skills that can be used in the lawyer-client collaboration. Lopez calls for the "professional" lawyer to recognize and encourage the use of the client's "lay" lawyering skills.[15]

Similarly, Lucie White characterizes conventional legal practice as "first-dimensional" lawyering, which does not address the most insidious aspects of subordination.[16] She advocates for third-dimensional lawyering, which involves "helping a group learn how to interpret moments of domination as opportunities for resistance."[17] According to White, the role of the lawyer is to help a group learn a method of deliberation that will lead to effective strategic action.[18]

By shifting the analysis away from results-oriented legal strategies and toward process-oriented client empowerment, both Lopez and White displace lawyers as the focal point of social change practice and offer a practical vision of how lawyers can achieve social change through community organizing.[19]

As a result of these critiques of conventional law reform models, scholars and activists began to seek alternative methods of social change practice that disfavored the traditional inclination of lawyers to resort to litigation as a means of achieving social change, and instead promoted community-based political action.

The law and organizing project flourishes only in the context of organized client constituencies. The law and organizing movement begins with the premise that building connections with community organizing campaigns is a critical component of social change advocacy. It highlights the value of organizing and questions the privileged position of lawyers within social movements. It defines success by asking whether legal advocacy has empowered organized client communities. It requires a type of lawyering that is intimately joined with grassroots organizing campaigns. This model reclaims the centrality of community members in shaping social change in which lawyers are ancillary. It encourages lawyers to deemphasize conventional legal practice and instead focus their efforts on facilitating community mobilization. While the requirement that the client be an organized community may be viewed as a limitation of the project, I argue that by forcing lawyers to value, encourage, and facilitate community organizing efforts, the project embodies the potential for lawyers to be part of the definition and implementation of a transformative agenda.

## Implementation of the Law and Organizing Project

The application of the law and organizing project will enable lawyers to avoid many of the detrimental effects of traditional lawyering. Demanding that the client be an organized community recognizes the importance and centrality of community organizing. Bill Quigley recommends that lawyers recognize the importance and necessity of community organizing.[20] For Quigley, lawyering involves not advocacy for individual interests, but advocacy with a group of people organized to reclaim what is rightfully theirs, their own power.[21] Encouraging organizing can have a transformative impact on the client's view of her entire life despite the legal outcome of the specific case. Similarly, according to Gabel and Harris, a lawyer should encourage community organizing when faced with a client.[22]

Similarly, Quigley advocates for the delawyering of the current systems so the members of the organization can better learn to advocate for themselves. The lawyer pursuing the goals of community empowerment is called to a higher form of advocacy than "doing for" her client. Rather, the lawyer is called to assist her client to escape the need of being anyone's client and instead help her learn to advocate for herself. This demands that the lawyer undo the secret wrappings of the legal system and share the essence of legal advocacy. Doing so lessens the mystical power of the lawyer.[23]

## Disfavoring Litigation

Given the evolution of the law and organizing project, which grew out of an increased emphasis on the primacy of mass mobilization and popular protest as the basis for political and economic change and an increased skepticism toward the inability of litigation to produce meaningful reform,[24] it seems logical that the law and organizing project disfavors the use of litigation.

I argue that the law and organizing project, by requiring the centrality and valuation of community organizing, prevents the lawyer from dominating the legal strategy with litigation. At the same time, by recognizing the need to maintain and facilitate the growth of community organizations, the law and organizing project must disfavor the use litigation since it often atomizes and individualizes struggles. As a result, the law and organizing project agrees with the common critique of cause lawyers' regular use of litigation.

If the lawyer values the role and power of community organizations, it is less likely that the lawyer will come to dominate the movement efforts. Moreover, if the lawyer identifies her role as an equal, if not subordinate, partner with her client community organization, and if she does not think she has superior knowledge, then she will listen to the needs and voices of the movement constituents and leaders before advancing litigation as the first priority. And in listening to voices that she perceives as being equally valuable and equally knowledgeable, it is less likely that her litigation propensities will survive to inhibit alternative movement by diverting concerns away from long-term projects such as grassroots mobilization, alliance-building, or more radical tactics such as public protest.

If the lawyer is committed to sustaining community organizing efforts that depend upon a vision of a unity, solidarity, and common cause among their constituents, then she is less likely to frame the movement goals in terms of disputes among discrete parties. She is less likely to be inclined to view litigation as the best strategy since it privileges individual controversies to the detriment of collective struggles and goals.

In sum, the lawyer of the law and organizing project will most often opt not to litigate. And if she does litigate, it is only after deciding to do so in partnership with the voices of the community.

## Organizing South Asian Domestic Workers

Many factors make organizing within an immigrant domestic worker community a particularly difficult task for organizers.[25] The realities of immigrant domestic workers present many conflicts with the traditional model of organizing. As a necessary result, lawyers working within the immigrant domestic worker community must be sensitive to these conflicts as they directly affect the success of the lawyering strategies employed.

In her article whose title is telling, yet a bit of an overstatement, *Organizing the Unorganizable: Private Paid Household Workers and Approaches to Employee Representation*,[26] Professor Peggie Smith lays out a number of the factors that make organizing domestic workers different from organizing within most other industries. Some of these factors include: 1) the one-on-one relationship between the employer and the domestic worker; 2) the job's location within the private sphere of the home; 3) the informality of the domestic service relationship; 4) the tenuousness of the domestic service relationship; 5) the difficulties of organizing immigrant workers; and 6. the lack of remedies available through the law. Organizing within the South Asian immigrant domestic worker context, due to the live-in nature of South Asian domestic work, presents yet more difficulties to organizing and adds another layer of difference from the traditional organizing model.

## One-on-One Relationship between Household Employer and Worker

Three aspects of the one-on-one relationship between the employer and worker inherent to domestic work present challenges to the use of the conventional "us-them" organizing strategy.[27] First, domestic workers must interact directly with their "clients"—the members of the household—who often include children, friends of the children, elders, family guests, and extended family members. As a result, the presence of these third parties complicates the conventional "us-them" view of workplace relations.[28]

Second, the personal relationship that develops between the domestic worker and her employer as a result of working in such close and constant proximity to each other adds a layer of emotional and interpersonal dynamics that obscures the conventional "us-them" view of workplace relations.[29] In the South Asian immigrant context, most domestics are hired for the purpose of tending to children and elder family members. These immigrant families often prefer South Asian domestics for the purpose of "acculturating" their U.S.-born children. One worker was forced to give the children Punjabi (a South Asian dialect) lessons and lessons in Sikh religion. Similarly, there is a desire to keep the "food of the country" in the household for the sake of educating the children and satisfying the rigid palates of elder family members.

Moreover, most South Asian immigrant domestics have left their own children behind. As a result, a very deep emotional bond develops between them and the children, especially when the relationship involves an infant. A loving relationship develops that often sustains the domestic worker, further complicating the "us-them" view of their workplace. For example, Rekha Mehra, domestic worker and core organizer of Workers' Awaaz, explains that since she has been working with her employer for six years, she has a very strong relationship with the youngest son. She feels like he is her son. He takes care of her when she is tired and is concerned if she ever gets hurt. She is very attached to him. Similarly, Madhu Bala is also a domestic worker and core organizer of Workers' Awaaz. Madhu had been working with the same employer for five years. When asked about her relationship with the children, she responds, "I love them; and they love me. The older son even helped me with my immigration papers and 'gives me five' all the time!" As a result, confronting the employer takes on a whole new complexity; at least one member of Workers' Awaaz has expressed her discomfort with protesting in front of the home of the children she loved.

Third, the majority of South Asian domestic workers find their jobs through newspaper ads in South Asian newspapers or through the friends or extended family of their past or current employer. References from past employers become more important given the lack of other formal evaluating procedures. Very few South Asian domestic workers go through an agency or any other mechanism that would put them in touch with other workers. This individualized job search process further hinders the formation of the "us" in the traditional "us-them" organizing strategy.

## Private Sphere of the Home

The one-on-one relationship between domestic workers and their employers described above develops at the worksite: the private homes of their employers. In the South Asian context, the majority of domestic workers are live-in workers. This is generally the case since most are recent immigrants from South Asia and do not have a permanent place to live in the United States. Shahbano Aliani, core organizer of Workers'

Awaaz in New York, states, "A large proportion of South Asian domestics are live-in. Most are women, and they think it is safer for them to have a place to live. It is also the expectation of employers for whom it is really convenient, so it becomes what *they* need—instead of saying they want twenty-four-hour help, they can say they want a live-in domestic worker. They will often couch it in terms of wanting the worker to be 'part of the family.'" Furthermore, the majority of ads for domestic workers in South Asian newspapers ask for live-in domestic help.

The location of domestic workers in the homes of their employers presents another layer of challenges to the traditional model of organizing in four ways. First, the private homes of the employer are small and geographically decentralized worksites. Working apart from one another, each dealing with their own separate employer, it is difficult for domestic workers to contact each other as workers in large factories can do. Most South Asian domestic workers work seven days a week. Few are lucky enough to get one day off. A constant struggle for Workers' Awaaz is membership attendance at meetings. The problem is exacerbated when we try to work in coalition with worker groups in other industries; domestic worker attendance at any trainings, workshops, and demonstrations held during the week is often impossible. The problem is further exacerbated in the South Asian immigrant worker context where modes of public transportation are often unfamiliar, daunting, or too far away—requiring the reluctant employer to drive her to the bus stop or train station. These issues present a severe challenge to traditional organizing, which depends heavily on a group of workers employed at a common job site for a single employer, such that both the employer and the bargaining unit are easily identifiable.[30]

Second, working in such close proximity to their employer, it is often too difficult to hide their involvement in organizing, and workers often refrain from organizing in order to prevent provoking their fearful employer. One member lost three jobs in six months for making and receiving Workers' Awaaz related phone calls. A number of our members have cell phones or pagers in order to prevent their employer from knowing that they are involved in Workers' Awaaz. Moreover, when a worker whose involvement in Workers' Awaaz has been exposed to the employer, it is often the case that her employer threatens to "warn" a future employer if asked to give a reference. Given the importance of references in the South Asian domestic worker industry, such a threat carries tremendous weight. As a result, they rarely have the opportunity to forge a sense of solidarity or develop a collective consciousness about ways to improve their labor conditions.

Third, the location of domestic workers in the homes of their employers contributes to the all-consuming nature of domestic work. This is particularly the case in the live-in context. One member of Workers' Awaaz had to share a room with the one-year-old child. Not only did the presence of this child in her room rob her of any personal space, the infant also disturbed her sleep with repeated cries for attention, which she was expected to provide, extending the length of her workday to twenty-four hours. Many immigrant domestic workers work, if not twenty-four-hour shifts, at minimum sixteen-hour days, seven days a week, with no breaks or vacations. As live-ins, South Asian domestic workers often have nowhere to go if they are given breaks. As a result, they remain at their worksite, as it is often their only source of shelter. Consequently they often lose their breaks due to a sense of obligation to work and an awkwardness from not working while at their workplace. For example, Madhu Bala states, "On my day off, even if I have nothing to do, or nowhere to go—if there is no Awaaz meeting—I will go roam around the neighborhood all day. I do not want [my employer] to get used to having me around; and whenever I have stayed, I end up cooking or cleaning anyway—it just doesn't feel right to rest while my employer cooks." As a result, such work leaves South Asian domestics with no personal space[31] or free time to devote to organizing for change.[32]

Fourth, as a result of the isolated nature of domestic work, there is a lack of exposure to organizing and to union activity. Moreover, Professor Smith suggests that since unions have historically privileged the needs of white male workers, they have hindered effective organizing within the service industry as women of color are disproportionately represented among low-wage service jobs.[33] Accordingly, women of color have long existed on the margin of organized labor's agenda.[34] As a consequence, the lack of familiarity with union organizing often undermines traditional union strategies that are based on the presumption that workers have knowledge of and experience with unions. As Shabano Aliani states, "Most of the women who end up working here, either didn't work in their home countries or worked in industries which are not usually organized. That is why they often don't know about unions and organizing as workers."

## Informality of Domestic Service Relationship

The informality of the domestic worker relationship with her employer often leaves workers vulnerable to abuse and subject to the whims of employers. Usually the terms and conditions of employment that are agreed upon take the form of verbal discussions consisting of vague oral promises.[35] For South Asian domestic workers, payments are often promised to be made to family members living in the home country of the worker. Frequently the payments are made in their conversion into South Asian currency, and the worker's passport is retained by the employer as a condition of employment and later used as blackmail if the worker wants to leave. The worker is told she will have to take care of a family of four, and then the family size grows as more members arrive from out of town. Oftentimes the domestic worker is "farmed out" to other family members or family friends who need her services.

A number of groups have been trying to create a standard domestic worker contract for individual domestic workers to use at the time of being hired.[36] However, the existence of such contracts do not account for the intimidation and desperation associated with the job search process and the problem of enforceability in the private homes where domestic workers' work looms large.[37] Shahenshah Begum, core organizer of Workers' Awaaz describes, "Such a contract may work with employers who know the laws, but most of the employers don't know the laws—maybe only 2 percent know the laws. Employers will choose the newer, more vulnerable workers. They will not choose a strong worker who they think knows her rights." In any event, the absence of an enforceable formal contract conflicts with traditional organizing that often challenges the terms of a defective and exploitative contract.

## Tenuous Relationship

Domestic workers often lack long-term attachments to a particular employer. Faced with extremely low wages, a lack of benefits, and unpredictable employment situations, domestic workers are constantly looking for new jobs.[38] In the South Asian immigrant worker context, most employers decide to hire with the introduction of small children into the family. Once the children have grown, the need for the domestic often disappears. This adds to the limited job security involved in the industry. *Workers' Awaaz* organizer Bala, for example, states, "When [my employers] first hired me, they said that they only needed me for two or three years because their children were getting older and so they wouldn't need me for that long." Organizer Shabano Aliani explains further, "The often high turnover rate in the South Asian domestic worker context is due to the job requirement associated with raising children, the personal nature of the job where people are bound to get on each others' nerves, and the sweatshop nature of the job." Moreover, in order to leave an exploitative workplace, they must already have another home to work in or be able to stay with a friend until they can secure a new job. Consequently, immigrant domestic workers are often constantly engaged in the job search process and constantly changing employers. According to Workers' Awaaz organizer Begum, "If it's a good job, then workers won't look for another job. But due to not getting enough money, suffering from employer abuse, and in concern for their own safety, some workers will try to change in six months or even in three months . . . in one year, a worker could have up to three or four jobs. Also, employers often like to keep changing workers so they can keep their payments to workers as low as possible as long as possible." The lack of long-term relationships with employers poses a challenge to the strategies of industrial unionism that envisions the organization of workers on an employer-specific basis.

## Organizing Difficulties

Additional difficulties arise in organizing domestic workers that are unique to immigrant workers. First, there is the problem of worker loyalty. Many immigrant workers who entered this country to work did so in order to send money back to their home countries and who themselves do not plan to stay here permanently. Organizer Begum states, "There is the impression that a worker will get more money here and will be able to send more money back to her children in order to give her children a better life and education." For example, organizer Mehra describes her personal history: "I used to work for Pan Am Airlines in India, and when I heard that the company was going to end, I decided to come to America to provide more for my three kids, who were getting bigger. I planned to come for two years and then go back. Now I have been here for eight years." Workers whose primary goal is securing as many jobs as possible may not be as invested in organizing to transform domestic work into a skilled profession.

Second, there is the problem of the threat of deportation for undocumented immigrant workers. Such a threat often creates an unwillingness to organize and a sense of desperation that leads to working for the lowest wages.[39] Organizer Begum explains, "Many undocumented workers are scared to talk openly about their problems. They think that if they open their mouth, they will lose her job, go to jail, or have to go back to their country—maybe they won't even get the little money that they are already getting. A lot of undocumented workers will take whatever they can get." For example, domestic worker Bala says, "I used to hold back—I was afraid that I couldn't go to the doctor, learn English— I felt I couldn't raise my voice because of my immigration status—and my employers would use it to scare me. Even now, whenever I tell my story, I am afraid to use my name, give my address—it's always on my mind. Even in public protests, I will go, but I am always afraid of the police." The fear of losing a much needed job and the fear of deportation have traditionally compromised attempts to organize immigrant workers.[40] As Shabano Aliani explains,

> It is an additional struggle that the organizer has to take on—to confront a worker's fear that immigration status affects her legitimacy to the point of not fighting for her rights. It does make organizing within any immigrant community harder. In a worker's mind, immigration can become a big issue, and so instead of fighting against working conditions and really recognizing what the problems are, they will focus on immigration issues and make them worker issues. A lot of workers will say that their problems will go away if they had a green card—but the reality is, what will change—you will be able to travel, but nothing really changes. Because of the informal private nature of the job, employers don't really think they are "employers"; they never think they or their home will be subject to public scrutiny—or legal challenge. So if a worker doesn't have status, the employer will use it to exploit her, and if the worker does have status, they will still exploit her. It doesn't really make a concrete difference. The challenge of the organizer is to deal with the inflated fear of immigration status that infects the immigrant worker movement.

Finally, some women turn to domestic work in order to get sponsored and obtain legal permanent residency. Organizer Begum explains, "Actual sponsorship rarely happens. Most of the time employers just want to keep the worker hanging in order to keep the power over her. They have no intention to actually sponsor her." Workers who are promised sponsorship are more dependent on their employer and less likely to engage in acts that may jeopardize their chances of obtaining permanent residency status.[41] Organizer Aliani explains, "When a worker is being sponsored by her employer, it is basically like bonded labor. When someone is in that kind of a contract, or in the hope of getting into that contract, they are much less likely to speak out."

## Absence of Legal Remedies

The lack of legal remedies available to immigrant domestic workers not only affects organizing and lawyering efforts within the domestic worker context, but also makes clear the failure to conceptualize domestic work as a legitimate occupation.

Historically, domestic service workers were denied workplace rights under the Fair Labor Standards Act (FLSA),[42] the National Industrial Recovery Act (NIRA),[43] the Social Security Act (SSA),[44] as well as the NLRA.[45] While today's paid household workers have been brought under the aegis of the SSA and the FLSA,[46] certain domestic workers continue to be exempted from the FLSA's overtime pay provision, which requires employers to pay employees overtime pay at the rate of one and one-half times the regular wage for hours worked in excess of forty in any single workweek.[47] This overtime pay requirement does not apply to "any employee who is employed in domestic service in a household and who resides in such household.[48] Given the fact that most immigrant domestic workers who are "imported" from their homeland reside in the household of their employer, the FLSA exemption for live-in domestic workers severely disadvantages immigrant workers.[49]

## The Exclusion from Collective Bargaining Statutes

By enacting the NLRA, Congress explicitly recognized the inequality of bargaining power between employees and employers as well as the need for employees to join forces as a means to balance that inequality. Congress's exclusion of domestic workers from state and federal collective bargaining statutes[50] should not only highlight the invisibility of domestic workers,[51] but it should also make clear the need to deconstruct the forces at play that obscure the reality of domestic work. Smith gives a number of explanations for the exclusion of domestic workers from state and federal collective bargaining statutes, including: 1) the NLRA was conceived with trade workers in mind who labor for a common employer and at a common work site, and domestic service sharply counters the collective ideology of the NLRA as well as the act's concerted action requirement; and 2) there is the belief that domestic service workers simply did not need the protections afforded by the NLRA. This view rests on an assumption that the home shields paid household workers from the ills associated with industrial life such that they do not require collective bargaining rights.[52] Immigrant domestic workers, more than any other group of workers, are especially vulnerable to exploitation, and the need for solidarity in this community is all the more vital. Accordingly, Smith argues that including private paid household workers within the coverage of state collective bargaining statutes should be a part of an overall strategy that will enable workers to participate actively in shaping their work experiences.

## Developing Successful Organizing Efforts

Given the particular nature of South Asian domestic work and the nature and history of organizing the South Asian domestic worker community, the role of community organizations is all the more vital and integral to mobilizing this group of workers. Therefore, lawyers working with this community must see as part of their role, the support and development of such organizations. As argued above, pushing for the expansion of the concept of collective representation to include the representation of community organizations, deemphasizing conflicts of interest and difficulties in discerning the interests of members of community groups, and finding alternatives to the adversarial model of our legal system are ways that lawyers can support organizing efforts while also addressing the immediate needs of individuals.

Avoiding litigation would be a more concrete way for lawyers to support organizing within the South Asian domestic worker community. Litigation often serves to pull the worker out of the organization and, after the case, leaves the organization with both a feeling of betrayal and a sense that the organization's mission is solely a service-providing one and not an organizing one.[53]

Other options for lawyers include pushing for policy legislative reform that would serve the needs of the immigrant worker community, that is, reforming the workers' compensation system for injured workers, supporting legislation to put a cap on overtime, or advocating for legislation that provides tax credit for child care. All of these strategies represent concrete ways of legitimizing women's work.

Within the litigation context, there are ways for lawyers to support organizing. For example, the lawyer can request that members of the organization be present at depositions and court appearances.[54] This not only gives the plaintiff worker more support, but allows for the perception that the case is not just about the injustice done to one worker, but about the injustices that are preventing a larger worker movement from forming. The lawyer can be present at public demonstrations that are part of the legal case, and be part of the planning and poster-making.[55] Again, this breaks down the perception that the lawyer provides a service only to the individual worker.

When conflicts arise between the plaintiff worker and other members of the organization, the lawyer should attempt to have a dialogue with the organization about the conflict before adhering to her duty of loyalty to her client.[56] In the absence of rules of ethics that are relevant to collaborative community lawyering, lawyers should try to re-conceive of the notion of "their client."

## Conclusion

The application of the law and organizing project enables lawyers to avoid the detrimental effects of traditional lawyering by demanding that they recognize the centrality of community organizing as well as the nature and history of organizing within the community with whom they seek to work. Such a recognition helps lawyers shift power to their client community, transforming their own role and the role of their client. Putting community organizations at the center also forces lawyers to disfavor litigation as the primary legal strategy. The expansion of the concept of collective representation to include the representation of community organizations, the deemphasis of conflicts of interest and difficulties in discerning the interests of members of community groups, and the abandonment and/or reform of the adversarial model of our legal system represent three strategies that will help facilitate the law and organizing project:

The one-on-one relationship between household employer and employee, combined with the job's location within the private sphere of the home and its casual nature, have led many to regard domestic workers as a community that defies organization. However, the growth of domestic worker organizations provides a powerful counter to that notion.[57] The difficulties in organizing domestic workers should rather lead to a recognition of the importance and success of such organizing efforts and to the impetus to support and sustain such efforts.

Achieving solidarity among paid domestic workers requires a new vision of organizing unimagined by the framers of the NLRA. It will require a commitment and willingness from individual workers, statutory reform, a change in the cultural valuation of domestic work, community organization,[58] and a method of lawyering that is sensitive to the nature of domestic work, the history of organizing in the domestic worker industry, and needs of the domestic worker community.

## Notes

1. See, for example, Steve Bachmann, *Lawyers, Law, and Social Change*, 13 N.Y.U. Rev. L. & Soc. Change 1, 4 (1984–85) (stating that "[o]rganized masses of people, not lawyers, play the critical roles [in social change], and the significant victories (or losses) occur outside the sphere of law").

2. See Gary Bellow and Jeanne Kettleson, *From Ethics to Politics: Confronting Scarcity and Fairness in Public Interest Practice*, 58 B.U. L. Rev. 337, 384 n.182 (1978) ("Unless public interest lawyers find ways of pursuing shorter term legal gains without encouraging dependency and blunting both individual and organized client initiatives to deal with their own problems, they will substantially undermine the possibility of the sorts of political activity essential to any long term resolution of the inequities that burden their clients."); see also Stephen Wexler, *Practicing Law for Poor People*, 79 Yale L.J. 1049, 1053 (1970) ("[T]he lawyer must seek to strengthen existing organizations of poor people and to help poor people start organizations where none exist").

3. Workers' Awaaz focuses on domestic workers, but our membership is open to workers in other industries. We are committed to building a base of workers in our community to come together with other workers in New York City and the U.S. to fight for our rights to a living wage, for freedom from long hours, and for healthy and safe working conditions.

4. Scott L. Cummings and Ingrid Eagly, *A Critical Reflection on Law and Organizing*, 48 UCLA L. Rev. 443 (2001) (discussing a new community-based approach to progressive lawyering that combines legal advocacy and grassroots action in a form of practice that Cummings and Eagly term "law and organizing"). Law and organizing includes varied practical strategies and has been given many names, including "rebellious lawyering," "empowerment lawyering," "change-oriented lawyering," "third dimensional lawyering," "collaborative lawyering," and "community lawyering." An extensive amount of legal scholarship has been associated with the emerging law and organizing model. See, for example, Angelo N. Ancheta, *Community Lawyering*, 81 Cal. L. Rev. 1363 (1993), Joel F. Handler, *Social Movements and the Legal System: A Theory of Law Reform and Social Change* (1978); Gerald P. Lopez, *Rebellious Lawyering: One Chicano's Vision of*

*Progressive Law Practice* (1992); Michael W. McCann, *Rights at Work: Pay Equity Reform and the Politics of Legal Mobilization* (1984); Richard Abel, *Lawyers and the Power to Change*, 7 Law & Policy 5, 8–9 (1985); Gary L. Blasi, *Litigation on Behalf of the Homeless: Systematic Approaches*, 31 Wash. U. J. Urb. & Contemp. L. 137 (1987); Raymond H. Brescia et al., *Who's in Charge, Anyway? A Proposal for Community-Based Legal Services*, 25 Fordham Urb. L.J. 831 (1998); Luke W. Cole, *Empowerment as the Key to Environmental Protection: The Need for Environmental Poverty Law*, 19 Ecology L.Q. 619 (1992); Michael J. Fox, *Some Rules for Community Lawyers*, 14 Clearinghouse Rev. 1 (1980); Jennifer Gordon, *We Make the Road by Walking: Immigrant Workers, the Workplace Project, and the Struggle for Social Change*, 30 Harv. C.R.-C.L. L. Rev. 407 (1995); Muhammad I. Kenyatta, *Community Organizing, Client Involvement, and Poverty Law*, Monthly Rev., Oct. 1983, at 18; Karl E. Klare, *Toward New Strategies for Low-Wage Workers*, 4 B.U. Pub. Int. L.J. 245 (1995); Richard Klawiter, *¡La Tierra Es Nuestra! The Campesino Struggle in El Salvador and a Vision of Community-Based Lawyering*, 42 Stan. L. Rev. 1625 (1990); Ascanio Piomelli, *Appreciating Collaborative Lawyering*, 6 Clinical L. Rev. 427 (2000); William P. Quigley, *Reflections of Community Organizers: Lawyering for Empowerment of Community Organizations*, 21 Ohio N.U. L. Rev. 455 (1995); Ann Southworth, *Collective Representation for the Disadvantaged: Variations in Problems of Accountability*, 67 Fordham L. Rev. 2449 (1999); Julie A. Su, *Making the Invisible Visible: The Garment Industry's Dirty Laundry*, 1 J. Gender, Race & Just. 405 (1998); Lucie E. White, *Mobilization on the Margins of the Lawsuit: Making Space for Clients to Speak*, 16 N.Y.U. Rev. L. & Soc. Change 535 (1987–88) [hereinafter White 1]; Lucie E. White, *To Learn and Teach: Lessons from Driefontein on Lawyering and Power*, 1988 Wis. L. Rev. 699 [hereinafter White 2].

5. See, for example, Klawiter *supra* note 4, at 1681–83 (stating that "courts have little power [and, increasingly, less willingness] to ameliorate or eliminate systemic abuses" and "are reluctant [if they were ever prone] to endorse and order redistributive measures"); Richard Delgado and Jean Stefancic, *Failed Revolutions: Social Reform and the Limits of Legal Imagination* (1994) (analyzing the limits of achieving social reform through law); Handler, *supra* note 18, at 232–33 (arguing that law reform efforts are incapable of producing fundamental social change); Michael W. McCann, *Taking Reform Seriously: Perspectives on Public Interest Liberalism* 200 (1986) ("Legal tactics not only absorb scarce resources that could be used for popular mobilization . . . [but also] make it difficult to develop broadly based, multi-issue, grass-roots associations of sustained allegiance."); Gerald N. Rosenberg, *The Hollow Hope: Can Courts Bring about Social Change?* 341 (1991) (advancing the concept of a *"Constrained Court"* model that assumes that the courts are inherently unable to produce significant social change due to three institutional constraints: "(i) the binding limitations of legal precedents and rights traditions; (ii) the lack of judicial independence from other government branches and public opinion; and (iii) the judiciary's restricted institutional capacity for developing and implementing effective social policies").

6. For a discussion of the critique of litigation, see McCann and Silverstein, *Rethinking Law's "Allurements": A Relational Analysis of Social Movement Lawyers in the Unites States*; see also Quigley, *supra* note 4, at 468 ("One of the weaknesses of litigation is the inherent limitation of the judicial system when called upon

to produce social reform"); Klawiter, *supra* note 4, at 1681–83 (noting that "conventional litigation approaches limit the tools for fighting injustice" because decisions often are not implemented, the beneficiaries often are unaware of the outcomes, or the decisions "fail to challenge institutional structures and cognitive faculties that sustain subordination"). See also Derrick Bell, foreword, *The Civil Rights Chronicles*, 99 Harv. L. Rev. 4, 24 (1985) ("[R]eal progress can come only through tactics other than litigation"); Aryeh Neier, *Only Judgment: The Limits of Litigation in Social Change* 19 (1982) ("[Litigation] is an effort that is probably doomed to fail and that should fail unless judges can be persuaded that compelling principles of corrective justice require them to enter territory ordinarily outside their province"); Rosenberg, *supra* note 5 (arguing that social reformers often succumb to the "lure of litigation" rather than providing real political reform).

7. See Rosenberg, *supra* note 5 (Rosenberg asserts that entire movements routinely fall prey to the "lure of litigation" as legal tactics favored by lawyers function like "fly paper," attracting and trapping movement advocates with their alluring logic of transformation).

8. Richard Abel has argued that litigation undermines social change movements by reinforcing poor clients' feelings of powerlessness and dispersing social conflict into individualized legal claims in which disputants are treated as atomized individuals. See Abel *supra* note 4 at 8–9; Richard L. Abel, introduction to *The Politics of Informal Justice* 1, 6–7 (Richard L. Abel, ed., 1982); Richard L. Abel, *Conservative Conflict and the Reproduction of Capitalism: The Role of Informal Justice*, 9 Int'l J. Soc. L. 245 (1981).

9. McCann and Silverstein, *supra* note 6 at 263.

10. See White 1, *supra* note 4 at 543–44; see also Klawiter, *supra* note 4, at 1682.

11. See Gordon, *supra* note 4, at 438–39. In 1998 the Campaign against Domestic Servitude of Workers' Awaaz began working with a domestic worker, Ms. Kaur, who was fired from her job for refusing to cook for a party of twenty-five. (See Workers Awaaz Press Release, "Women Workers Protest against Domestic Servitude," August 3, 2000.) She became involved with Workers' Awaaz, and together, along with the National Employment Law Project and the NYU Immigrant Rights Clinic, they filed a federal lawsuit against the employer family, seeking a total of $70,000 for unpaid wages and compensatory damages. Soon after a public demonstration in front of Beth Israel Hospital (where the mother worked) that was organized by Workers' Awaaz and Ms. Kaur, a $50,000 settlement was reached in court, with no gag order. See Steven Kreytak, "Ex-Housekeeper Sues Doctors," *Newsday* August 9, 2000; Viji Sundaram, "Activists Protest Alleged Abuse of N.Y. Maid," *India West* August 18, 2000 at A1. However, the process of litigation, the numerous and tedious meetings in preparation for depositions and discovery requests, effectively took Ms. Kaur out of the organization. Unable to attend meetings with the lawyers as well as with the organization, she began to feel more distanced from the members. After the settlement was reached, Ms. Kaur no longer remained active with the organization; and the members felt at worst, betrayed, and at best, they felt that the role of organization was merely to provide a service to workers as opposed to organizing them.

12. See Klawiter, *supra* note 4, at 1681 (arguing that litigation "contributes to the very subordination it purports to remedy"). See also Quigley, *supra* note 4, at 467 (stating that litigation does not usually further the goal of empowerment and should

therefore be avoided because it is potentially "harmful to the growth and development of [a community] organization").

13. The most influential scholars in this regard have been Gerald Lopez and Lucie White.

14. See generally Ancheta, *supra* note 4.

15. Lopez, *supra* note 4 at 30–82.

16. White 2, *supra* note 4 at 755–57.

17. Ibid. at 763.

18. Ibid. at 764; see also Lucie E. White, *Collaborative Lawyering in the Field? On Mapping the Paths from Rhetoric to Practice*, 1 Clinical L. Rev. 157 (1994), at 157 (stating that "third-dimensional" lawyering "seeks to enable poor people to see themselves and their social situation in ways that enhance their world-changing powers").

19. See Cummings and Eagly, *supra* note 4 at 460.

20. For arguments that advocate actively enlisting client groups in the struggle for social reform, see Lopez, *supra* note 4 at 47–56 (discussing how to foster collaboration between lawyers and community members as "co-eminent practitioners" of social change); Quigley, *supra* note 4 at 456. (Quigley asserts: "In fact, if an organization could only have one advocate and had to choose between the most accomplished traditional lawyer and a good community organizer, it had better, for its own survival, choose the organizer.") See also Stephen Ellmann, *Client-Centeredness Multiplied: Individual Autonomy and Collective Mobilization in Public Interest Lawyers' Representation of Groups*, 78 Va. L. Rev. 1103, 1106 (1992) ("The success of [legal] strategies . . . may depend on the extent to which [public interest lawyers] empower clients outside as well as inside the courts, and so may hinge on the degree to which they transform this multiplicity of people into a group"); Alan W. Houseman, *Community Group Action: Legal Services, Poor People and Community Groups*, 19 Clearinghouse Rev. 392, 400 (1985) ("[N]ew relationships must be forged with poor people's groups—both existing groups and those that are newly emerging"); see Abel, *supra* note 4 at 8–9 (claiming that the "law must be subordinated to other modes of activism" and highlighting examples of lawyers working with organizers as "achievements that could inspire and guide future efforts").

21. See Quigley, *supra* note 4 at 471–473.

22. Peter Gabel and Paul Harris in "Building Power and Breaking Images," 291–300 in *LAWYERS: A Critical Reader* (Richard Abel, ed.). The example used is in the landlord-tenant context.

23. Quigley, *supra* note 4 at 477.

24. See *supra* note 6 and accompanying text.

25. See Jean Collier Brown, *Domestic Workers and Unions*, 45 Am. Federationist 477, 477 (1938). ("Domestic workers, seeking to organize, face more serious obstacles than do workers in almost any other industry or trade.")

26. Peggie Smith, *Organizing the Unorganizable: Private Paid Household Workers and Approaches to Employee Representation*, 79 N.C.L. Rev 45 (2000) [hereinafter Smith].

27. See also Dorothy Sue Cobble, *Union Strategies for Organizing and Representing the New Service Workforce*, 43 Indus. Rel. Res. Ass'n Ann. Proc. 76, 81 (1990) ("In many workplaces, the older 'us against them' model that assumes hostility

and rigid demarcations between labor and management no longer suits workers or their bosses").

28. The typical newspaper advertisement for a South Asian domestic worker involves the responsibility of taking care of at least one child.

29. See, for example, Evelyn Nakano Glenn, *Issei, Nisei, War Bride: Three Generations of Japanese American Women in Domestic Service* (1986), at 154 (stating that workers have "access to the most intimate regions of the household and might become privy to family secrets").

30. John Howley, *Justice for Janitors: The Challenge of Organizing in Contract Services*, Lab. Res. Rev., spring 1990, at 61, 64–65.

31. Aliani interview, *supra* note 58. ("There is no personal space—no personal time—they are always at work.")

32. See *Why Is the Household Employee So Heavily Out-Weighed in the Scale of Security? Household Occupation in the District of Columbia* (Washington League of Women Shoppers, Washington, D.C.) [n.d.], at 8 (Watson Papers, Folder 6.40, Catherwood Library, Cornell School of Industrial Labor Relations) (noting that paid household workers have limited bargaining power and little time to devote to organizing); see also Glenn, *supra* note 54 at 141 (observing that residential domestic service left domestic workers with little time for their own families or outside social relationships); David Katzman, *Seven Days a Week: Women and Domestic Service in Industrializing America* 177, 112–13 (1978) (discussing the lack of quality time enjoyed by live-in domestics); Peggie Smith, *Regulating Paid Household Work: Class, Gender, Race, and Agendas of Reform*, 48 Am. U. L. Rev. 851, 871 (1999) (noting that employers demanded full-time allegiance from live-in workers, expecting them to work around the clock).

33. Smith, *supra* note 51 at 71. Based on 1999 statistics, 95 percent of all private household workers are women, 15 percent are black, and 29 percent are Latina. Bureau of Labor statistics, U.S. Department of Labor, Household Data Annual Averages, Emp. & Earning, January 2000, at 166, 180 tb 1.11; see also Mary Romero, *Maid in the U.S.A.* 71 (1992) (observing that "minority and immigrant women are overrepresented in [domestic service]"). *See also* Doreen J. Mattingly, *Job Search, Social Networks, and Local Labor-Market Dynamics: The Case of Paid Household Work in San Diego, California*, 20 Urb. Geography 46, 52 (1999) (observing the dominance of immigrant women, many of whom are undocumented, in the San Diego market for domestic service); Stuart Silverstein, "Domestics: Hiring the Illegal Hits Home," *Los Angeles Times*, October 28, 1994, at A1 (noting that in California, 1990 figures indicate that one in three domestics were undocumented).

34. See Jacqueline Jones, *Labor of Love, Labor and Sorrow* 147 ("As blacks, females, and unskilled workers, the vast majority of southern black women have no role to play in trade unions dominated by white men"); see also Philip S. Foner, *Women and the American Labor Movement: From the First Trade Unions to the Present* 99–100 (1982) (observing that women workers generally, because they were considered unskilled relative to men, did not fit into the agenda of the American Federation of Labor [AFL]).

35. See Hondagneu-Sotelo, *Regulating the Unregulated?: Domestic Workers' Social Networks*, 41 Soc. Prob. 53 (stating that the final negotiation between employer and worker occurs "without the benefit of guidelines established by government, unions, employment agencies or private firms").

36. Domestic Workers United and the Women Workers Project of the Committee Against Anti-Asian Violence (CAAAV) in New York City has been working to develop a standard employment contract that provides decent working conditions for domestic workers.

37. Aliani interview, *supra* note 58 ("There is already labor law which is enforceable in a court of law, and which is not being enforced. What more would such a contract provide—how useful would it be? In the South Asian context, we already seen conditions deteriorating—if a worker walks in with a contract, no one will listen to her—how do you enforce it? Does it become a he-said, she-said? Why create another mechanism that will not be enforced? Therefore, it is not a good organizing tool because it will demoralize workers. As an organizing tool, it should provide a concrete legal advantage over existing labor law, or else it should be easier to enforce. At least the short term goals should achievable— like a settlement").

38. For a discussion of the need among paid household workers to engage in a constant job search, see Hondagneu-Sotelo, *supra* note 59; Julianne Malveaux, "From Domestic Worker to Household Technician: Black Women in a Changing Occupation," in *Black Women in the Labor Force* 85, 87 (Phyllis Wallace, ed., 1980); Leslie Salzinger, "A Maid by Any Other Name: The Transformation of 'Dirty Work' by Central American Immigrants," in *Ethnography Unbound: Power and Resistance in the Modern Metropolis* 139, 143 (Michael Burawoy et al., eds., 1991).

39. Immigration issues may affect a worker's acceptance of exploitative work conditions in other ways. See also Viji Sundaram, "Activists Protest Alleged Abuse of N.Y. Maid," *India West,* August 18, 2000, at A1 ("Ms. Kaur stuck with her employer for so long because she had filed for naturalization and was using their address in all her communications with the Immigration and Naturalization Service").

40. See also Cecilia Garza, "Foreign Domestics: The Use and Abuse of Undocumented Household Workers," *4 Race, Gender & Class: An Interdisciplinary & Multicultural Journal* 64, 67 (1997) (noting undocumented domestics' concerns about the possibility of deportation); Cory Fisher, "When a House Is Not a Home: Domestic Workers on the Westside Band Together to Preserve Their Rights," *Los Angeles Times*, December 31, 1999 (*Westside Weekly*) at 1 (noting that "many undocumented domestics choose not to speak out regarding their mistreatment because they and their families could face deportation").

41. Shellee Colen, "'Housekeeping' for the Green Card: West Indian Household Workers, the State, and Stratified Reproduction in New York," in *At Work in Homes, Household Workers in World Perspective* 89, 98–99 (Roger Sanjek and Shellee Colen, eds., 1990).

42. The Fair Labor Standards Act (FLSA) of 1938, 29 U.S.C.A. 201–219 (West 1998 and Supp. 2000), entitles covered employees to minimum wages and overtime pay.

43. The National Industrial Recovery Act (NIRA) of 1933, ch. 90, 48 Stat. 195, enables industries to establish codes of fair competition to regulate the wages and hours of workers in those industries and gives employees the right to organize and engage in collective bargaining. Although not explicitly excluded from the NIRA, the National Recovery Administration concluded that the act did not reach domestic service workers.

44. The Social Security Act of 1935, 42 U.S.C. 301–1397f (1994 and Supp. 1998) created a series of entitlement programs including unemployment insurance, old-age pensions, and aid to dependent children.

45. The National Labor Relations Act of 1935, 29 U.S.C. 151–169 (1994) grants covered employees the right to organize and engage in collective bargaining.

46. Provisions of the Social Security Act and Fair Labor Standards Act were extended to paid household workers in 1950 and 1974 respectively.

47. 29 U.S.C. 207(a)(1) (1994 and Supp. IV 1998).

48. Ibid. at 213(b)(21).

49. The majority of South Asian domestic workers are live-in workers who came to the U.S. to pursue a live-in job. Leaving their own home and family behind, their first housing arrangement in the U.S. was their first job. See *infra* note 58.

50. It is important to point out that the NLRA's exclusion of domestic service workers from coverage arguably does not preclude protection under state laws. However, most state collective bargaining statutes have followed the NLRA, explicitly excluding these workers from coverage. California is an exception to this trend.

51. See Smith, *supra* note 51 at 56 (discussing the invisibility of domestic work: "On a physical level, the domestic service relationship is invisible because it takes place within the private sphere of the home. Economically, the relationship is invisible because—similar to women's unpaid household labor—it defies market exchange terms. Situated inside the home and outside the purview of capital, domestic service is frequently regarded as unproductive labor based on the theory that it does not produce surplus value for capital. Because of its close association with women's unpaid household labor, and its connection with the intimacies of family life, domestic service has often been devalued as a form of real work").

52. See Smith, *supra* note 51 at 62–67.

53. See *supra* note 11.

54. The National Employment Law Project used such a strategy in a case involving a Workers' Awaaz member, Ms. Kaur. See *supra* note 11. This strategy was later referred to in a letter from the employer's lawyer as "intimidation tactics."

55. The National Employment Law Project lawyers made it a point not only to come to the Workers' Awaaz protest demonstration outside of Ms. Kaur's employer's workplace, but also to curtail Ms. Kaur's deposition in order to make it to the demonstration in time.

56. Out of deference to the rules of professional responsibility, Mike Wishnie of the NYU Immigrants Rights Clinic refused to talk to a core organizer about a worker's case due to a personality conflict that had arisen between his "client" and another member of the organization. Despite the fact that Wishnie had a preexisting, long-standing relationship with Workers' Awaaz, he felt that he had to be loyal only to his "client." Similarly fearful of such conflicts, Nancy Morawetz of the NYU Immigrants Rights Clinic instructed her law students not to communicate with any Awaaz members in the event that we would try to "control" their "client." As a result, their client was forced to pay for endless expensive phone calls made to Awaaz members in order to stay connected to the organization as she wanted to.

57. For an extensive list of domestic worker organizations throughout America, see *Rights Begin at Home: Protecting Yourself as a Domestic Worker* (on file with the National Employment Law Project in New York City). This handbook is geared toward the practical needs of domestic workers, outlining legal rights, suggesting

strategies that can be implemented in the face of limited statutory rights, and providing a list of resources including community organizations that organize domestic workers. This handbook is the product of a collaborative effort of the National Employment Law Project, Asian American Legal Defense and Education Fund, Workers' Awaaz, Andolan, and the Committee Against Anti-Asian Violence.

58. See, for example, Smith, *supra* note 51 at 81–82. Smith suggests the formation of worker-run cooperatives as a promising approach to organize domestic workers as it offers a means to improve their economic conditions without owing anything to the government or to employers.

## 9

SARU JAYARAMAN

# "ROCing" the Industry: Organizing Restaurant Workers in New York

On September 11, 2001, 73 workers lost their lives at Windows on the World, the restaurant at the top of the World Trade Center. All of the 73 workers were immigrants. Another 300 workers, also majority immigrant, lost their jobs from the same restaurant. The restaurant industry on the whole was devastated; in the months and weeks that followed the tragedy, another 13,000 restaurant workers lost their jobs as food service establishments shut down all over the city.

Quite unexpectedly, amidst all the tragedy, a powerful opportunity to change the nature of the industry itself and create a new movement for restaurant workers has emerged. Immediately following 9/11, the Hotel Employees Restaurant Employees (HERE) Local 100, New York's food service workers' union, received special funding and an outpouring of support to assist displaced workers and the families of the deceased workers. Realizing it did not have the capacity to provide ongoing support to these workers, HERE Local 100 asked three former Windows on the World workers and an organizer to head up the new effort; together, these four individuals created the Restaurant Opportunities Center of New York (ROC-NY).

What was initially intended as a temporary measure of support for displaced workers from the World Trade Center has become an immigrant worker–led center with its sights set on organizing the 99 percent of New York City's restaurant workforce that does not enjoy the benefits of a union. Our long-term vision is to change the balance of power in the industry by organizing restaurant workers around strategic industry campaigns. Using protests, media pressure, research, policy, and cooperative development, ROC-NY has organized restaurant workers citywide for improved working conditions.

## The Workers

ROC-NY's two-year analysis of the restaurant sector indicates that there are 165,000 restaurant workers in New York City, 67% of whom are immigrants from all over the world, and approximately 30% of whom are undocumented. At Windows on the World, for example, workers came from approximately thirty countries, including Mexico, the Dominican Republic, Ecuador, Colombia, El Salvador, Peru, Uruguay, Costa Rica, Brazil, Bangladesh, Senegal, Ghana, Ivory Coast, Jamaica, Pakistan, India, Yemen, Egypt, Haiti, China, Taiwan, Vietnam, Ireland, Morocco, Nepal, England, and Curacao. This mirrors the workforce in New York's food service industry, 70% of which is immigrants from Latin America, Africa, Asia, and the Arab world, and 10% of which is African American. A job in a restaurant can be the first step for many immigrants to financial security.

Too many of these restaurant workers are forced to work long hours for low wages in unhealthy, hazardous working conditions. Our recently completed restaurant industry report, *Behind the Kitchen Door: Pervasive Inequality in New York's Thriving Restaurant Industry*, demonstrated that working conditions in the industry are horrendous. Approximately 11% of all workers surveyed do not receive the minimum wage of $5.15 per hour, and 56% of all workers surveyed who work more than forty hours per week do not receive proper overtime payment. Approximately 50% reported that they had never received training on workplace safety; approximately 55% ranked their workplace health and safety conditions as "fair" or "poor"; 28% reported that they have been forced to do things that put their own health and safety at risk; 29% reported doing things on the job because they were under time pressure that put others' safety at risk; 45% reported that the kitchen in the restaurant where they worked gets unsafely hot; 36% reported fire hazards in the restaurant; and 37% reported being burned on the job. Clearly our research has highlighted the need for policy options that would improve workers' occupational safety and health.

Exploitation and racial discrimination permeate the industry: 32% of all workers surveyed reported experiencing verbal abuse on the basis of race, immigration status, and/or language, and 23% reported having been passed over for a promotion based on the same factor. In fact, in our employer interviews, several restaurant owners openly admitted to placing white workers in the front, highest-paying positions while relegating immigrants and workers of color to lower-paying and back-of-the-house positions.

As immigrants, some without legal status, these workers are vulnerable to exploitation and terrified to complain for fear of losing their job or, worse, being deported. In the last ten years, most individually owned tablecloth restaurants have merged into megarestaurant corporations that dominate the industry. Meanwhile, 99% of the workers in the industry continue to lack union support. Thus, restaurant corporations, already proliferating in New York City over the last ten years, have only become more powerful vis-à-vis their employees.

### Initial Victories

ROC-NY is the newest of approximately fifteen immigrant workers centers throughout New York City that organize the margins of the traditional labor movement. These workers centers have focused their efforts on populations the mainstream unions have not included in their organizing efforts. In the case of the restaurant industry, HERE Local 100's more than 5,000 members work mostly in corporate cafeterias; only 1,500 work in restaurants, and the focus of the union's restaurant expansion is fancy, tablecloth restaurants. No other institution in the city or, in fact, nationwide focuses exclusively on organizing restaurant workers to raise standards in the industry on the whole.

To this end, over the last three years ROC-NY has won six battles for restaurant worker collective power. In July 2002, ROC-NY organized workers from Windows on the World to pressure former Windows owner David Emil to hire thirty-two former Windows workers at his newly opened restaurant, Noche. Emil did not initially wish to hire his former employees for fear that they would form a union. Responding to ongoing pressure from ROC-NY members, Emil created an entirely new banquet department at Noche and hired several bussers, bartenders, and waiters he had previously refused to hire. Since that initial victory, through a combination of litigation, press, and protest, we have won more than $300,000 in back wages and discrimination claims for food service workers. At one Brooklyn deli we were able to win a $50,000 settlement for five undocumented workers owed for minimum wage and overtime back wages. At the Three Guys restaurant in uptown Manhattan, we have been able to win a settlement providing compensation for discrimination, paid vacations, paid sick days, promotions, the firing of an abusive waiter, and a posting in the restaurant guaranteeing workers the involvement of ROC-NY in the case of any future discrimination. Most recently, we won a tremendous victory against the Smith & Wollensky Restaurant Group, called a battle of "David and Goliath" proportions by *Crain's Business Weekly*. In this campaign, we won $164,000 for twenty-three workers in unpaid overtime wages and discrimination payments, as well as vacations, sick days, internal job postings, job security, an employee manual, and more. These battles have helped spread the word among restaurant workers that ROC-NY is a source of support; we have thus grown from a small organization of less than 100 members to a very large organization of more than 1,000 members.

## Organizing Programs

Five central components make up ROC-NY's fundamental activities: 1) conducting Workplace Justice Campaigns against New York restaurant corporations; 2) organizing the New York Restaurant Industry Coalition to complete exhaustive research on the industry and to introduce and pass legislation to raise industry standards; 3) opening cooperatively owned restaurants, in which workers each own equal shares of the business; 4) fighting for amnesty for undocumented workers; and 5) giving ongoing political education for restaurant worker members.

## Workplace Justice Campaigns

In early 2003, ROC-NY conducted a careful study of the various ownership groups in New York's restaurant industry. The industry's shift from individual ownership to conglomerate ownership encouraged us to consider restaurant corporations as targets. With such low union density in the restaurant sector, wages and working conditions are abysmally low industry-wide, and some union restaurants complain that high wages and benefits make them uncompetitive vis-à-vis the majority of their rivals. ROC-NY decided to pursue powerful corporate targets, thereby sending a message to the industry that one way or another—through ROC-NY, a union, or some alternative form—working conditions in the industry will be raised.

Throughout this process, ROC-NY's organizers were continuously conducting outreach in the target restaurants to include more and more workers in ROC-NY and in the campaign. Over time, ROC-NY is thus simultaneously organizing the individual restaurants in the restaurant corporations and building a large and ever-growing multi-workplace base that is poised to take on broader public policy campaigns for improved conditions for all restaurant workers in New York.

## Policy Campaign Based on Restaurant Research and Legislation

ROC-NY has just culminated a serious research process on the restaurant industry, publishing the ground-breaking report *Behind the Kitchen Door: Pervasive Inequality in New York City's Thriving Restaurant Industry*. We have created the New York Restaurant Industry Coalition, which includes academics, attorneys, economic development experts, unions, representatives of various political offices, worker and immigrant advocates, and workers. The report was based on quantitative analysis of official government data, 35 one-hour interviews with restaurant owners, 45 one-hour interviews with workers, and more than 530 surveys of workers, which we completed by training our members, restaurant workers, to follow their fellow workers home on subways after the night shift, conduct surveys with them, and tell them about ROC-NY. The surveys proved to be an extremely useful tool for outreach as well and have allowed a few legislators who are members of the Coalition to begin drafting particular legislation. We presented the report at our New York Restaurant Industry Summit in January 2005, an event that more than 250 people, including unions, restaurant owners, government officials, press, and others, attended. The report, the summit, and the consequent press certainly had an impact; as a result, three committees of the New York City Council held a joint hearing on "The State of Wages and Working Conditions for New York City Restaurant Workers, and Its Impact on the Public Health." The summit has also led to the creation of the Restaurant Industry Roundtable, our effort to engage "High-Road" employers in educating their fellow restaurateurs about their legal obligations, and encouraging them to understand the benefits of the "High Road."

Based particularly on the information that emerged from the five hundred worker surveys, certain legislators' offices that are part of the coalition have begun to draft a unique piece of legislation that would mandate that any restaurant owners who violate workers' rights would have their operating licenses revoked by the Department of Health. We are currently meeting with various public health groups and the Department of

Health to show how workers' rights and workers' health are public health issues; restaurant owners who violate labor laws and therefore negatively affect workers' health also are prone to violating the city's health code. Our recent survey of five hundred workers proves irrefutably that workers who suffer from not receiving the minimum wage and/or overtime wages work in the same restaurants that do not provide health and safety training to their workers, force their workers to work under heavy pressure that puts customers' health at risk, and include a number of fire and other safety hazards. This data thus proves that restaurant owners who violate labor laws are the same irresponsible restaurateurs who violate the health code.

ROC-NY's Policy Committee, comprised of restaurant workers, has met with city council members, hundreds of restaurant workers, and various organizations city-wide to educate them about policy options and restaurant working conditions. ROC-NY organizers train members of the Policy Committee to meet with individual legislators to educate them about the legislation and to speak at major events we organize on the issue. The committee had been instrumental in raising the New York State minimum wage, particularly for tipped workers, by targeting New York State Senate Labor Chair Olga Mendez and organizing several worker trips to the state capitol.

## Cooperative Restaurants Program (CRP)

Rather than simply presenting research on the restaurant industry and a single policy option, we will actually be opening a cooperatively owned restaurant that will serve as a model for the industry and create a new group of worker-owners who will advocate for workers' rights. The restaurant concept originated from the Windows on the World workers' desire to find decent employment after losing their jobs after September 11, 2001, and to create a legacy for their seventy-three lost brothers and sisters. After opening the restaurant in fall 2005, the program's work will focus on organizing the worker-owners to testify publicly in favor of workers' rights and worker-beneficial legislation and initiating a second group of workers to organize a second cooperative restaurant. The fundamental philosophy that guides the Cooperative Restaurants Program is our hope to create a model for the industry and create hundreds of new restaurant owners in New York City who are actually workers, who will support worker-beneficial legislation and counterbalance the restaurant industry's lobby. Throughout the process, we are organizing cooperative committee members—who are all immigrants—to attend public meetings and advocate for restaurant workers' rights.

Over the next several years, ROC-NY hopes to spearhead the development of several new cooperative restaurants in downtown Manhattan. These ventures will not only be opportunities for ownership and employment for hundreds of immigrant workers, but can also help change the balance of power within the industry. The presence of hundreds of worker-owners can serve as a powerful voice for better working conditions for workers and can also serve as an example to owners that having good working conditions can actually be profitable.

To achieve this vision with the first cooperative committee members, the CRP is: 1) conducting ongoing political education with cooperative committee members concerning the state of the industry and their role in changing it; and 2) seeking integration of the new worker-owners into the New York State Restaurant Association. The CRP draws material from ROC-NY's ongoing research study of the industry, to educate members of the Steering Committee about the state of the industry and the importance of their advocacy within it. This education will be absolutely essential to ensure that the worker-owners do not become typical restaurateurs, but instead serve as a voice for change. Once the restaurant is open, the CRP will seek inclusion of the worker-owners into the New York State Restaurant Association, which currently serves as a powerful industry lobby, and for audiences with the New York City Council's Economic Development Committee. These worker-owners can serve as a voice for workers' rights in both arenas.

After opening the first cooperative restaurant in 2005, we will begin to organize a second group of workers who wish to open a second cooperative restaurant, involving the first set of worker-owners in training the second group. As ROC-NY begins to introduce legislation to raise standards for restaurant workers, ROC-NY will initiate and open cooperative restaurants that serve as models for high-standard restaurants—demonstrating owners' ability to make profits while empowering their workers.

## Amnesty Campaign

Close to twenty families of victims and almost one hundred displaced workers from Windows on the World are undocumented. Many of the families—mostly now-single mothers—of the deceased came to the United States to claim their loved ones' remains and have chosen to stay in the country to build a new life for themselves and their children. These families have met with a number of political offices and media sources to win support for their cause, and are working in partnership with organizations such as the New York Immigration Coalition to meet with various legislators to seek options for amnesty. Based on these efforts, they have identified the U-Visa, a visa intended for victims of a crime, as a visa applicable to undocumented families of World Trade Center victims and workers who lost their jobs at the World Trade Center. They have thus formed a coalition of groups citywide to launch a campaign to win U-Visas for this population. Through the U-Visa application process, they have already obtained work authorization for three families, and now seek the same for the remaining seventeen.

To win the U-Visas, ROC-NY is organizing a campaign to win the public's support and the support of various political officials. A victory on this campaign for amnesty for a specific group will inspire the committee to continue the fight for amnesty for all immigrant workers.

## Organizing Philosophy: Lessons Learned

As the newest of approximately fifteen independent workers' centers in New York City and the nearly hundred such centers nationwide, ROC-NY has been able to learn much from more experienced worker center organizers and has also offered its own unique innovations to the movement.

One such innovation is our Workplace Justice Campaign activity. We have studied and mapped the industry thoroughly and seek to improve conditions in some of the city's best-known and most powerful restaurants, to send a message to the rest of the industry. ROC-NY campaigns serve two functions. First, the campaigns raise standards in the industry, particularly when industry leaders form public partnerships with an organization like ROC-NY. Second, the organizing campaigns assist us with outreach and create fertile ground for future legislative organizing.

A second unique aspect of ROC-NY is the research and policy work in which we are engaged. We sought to conduct the research to place ourselves as an alternative clearinghouse of information on the restaurant industry; until we came on the scene, the only source of data on the restaurant industry had been produced by the industry itself. We have sought to produce data that speaks to the reality of working conditions in the industry, and that is both produced by and accessible to restaurant workers themselves. We have been able to engage workers in conducting research on the industry by training them to conduct surveys with their fellow workers. The bill that has emerged directly from this research is also unique, because it is the first time a city license is being used to connect labor law and public health issues anywhere in the country. We hope that it will create a useful precedent to groups across the country and, most important, send a message to restaurant owners about the importance of complying with the law.

Finally, we are trying to not only expose the terrible working conditions in the industry, but also create a positive model for the industry. By opening a cooperatively owned restaurant, we are hoping to show employers that they can pay and treat their workers well and still make a profit. Principally, we feel we can transform the industry and the industry lobby with hundreds of new owners who are actually workers.

Ultimately, ROC-NY is organizing restaurant workers, primarily immigrants, to raise standards and improve working conditions in New York's restaurant industry. With the onslaught of globalization, we are mobilizing immigrant workers for greater power in the belly of the beast, New York City.

# References

AFL-CIO, Article XXI Decision, January 13, 2001.

Ahlburg, Dennis A. (August 1996): "Remittances and the Income Distribution in Tonga," *Population Research and Policy Review* 15(4):391–400.

Athukorala, Premachandra (1993): "Improving the Contribution of Migrant Remittances to Development: The Experience of Asian Labour-Exporting Countries," *International Migration* 31(1):103–24.

Bacon, David (January–February 2000): "Immigrant Workers Ask Labor 'Which Side Are You On?' *Working USA: The Journal of Labor and Society* 3 (5):7–18.

Bailey, Thomas, and Roger Waldinger (1991): "Economic Change and the Ethnic Division of Labor," in John Mollenkopf, ed., *The Dual City.* New York: Russell Sage Foundation.

Banerjee, B. (December 1984): "The Probability, Size, and Uses of Remittances from Urban to Rural Areas in India," *Journal of Development Economics* 16:293–311.

Barringer, H., and G. Kassebaum (1989): "Asian Indians as a Minority in the United States: The Effect of Education, Occupations, and Gender on Income," *Sociological Perspectives* 32(4):501–520.

Besley, Timothy (1995): "Nonmarket Institutions for Credit and Risk Sharing in Low-Income Countries," *Journal of Economic Perspectives* 9 (3):115–27.

Borjas, George (1995): "Assimilation and Changes in Cohort Quality Revisited: What Happened to Immigrant Earnings in the 1980s?" *Journal of Labor Economics* (April):201–45.

Brown, R. P. C. (1992): "Migrants' Remittances, Capital Flight, and Macroeconomic Imbalance in Sudan's Hidden Economy," *Journal of African Economies* 1(1):86–108.

Brown, Richard, (1995): *Consumption and Investments from Immigrants' Remittances in the South Pacific.* Geneva: Employment Department, International Labor Office.

Brown, Richard, and John Connell (October 1993): "The Global Flea Market: Migration, Remittances and the Informal Economy in Tonga," *Development and Change* 24(4):611–47.

Burki, Shahid Javed (Autumn 1984): "International Migration: Implications for Labor Exporting Countries," *Middle East Journal* 38(4):668–84.

Burney, Nadeem A. (Winter 1987): "Workers' Remittances from the Middle East and Their Effect on Pakistan's Economy," *Pakistan Development Review* 26(4):745–61.

Chaudhuri, Jayasri Ray (1993): *Migration and Remittances: Inter-Urban and Rural-Urban Linkages*. New York: Sage Publications.

Chicas Canales, Jose. Member of the Workplace Project and Leader of V.E.R. Interviewed by author, November 2001

Choucri, Nazli (June 1986): "The Hidden Economy: A New View of Remittances in the Arab World," *World Development* 14(6):697–712.

Connell, John (1980). *Remittances and Rural Development: Migration, Dependency, and Inequality in the South Pacific*. Canberra: Australian National University.

De la Cruz, Blanca E. (1997): *The Socioeconomic Dimensions of Remittances: A Case Study of Five Mexican Families*. http://www.aad.berkeley.edu/95journal/blancadelacruz.html.

Díaz-Briquets, Sergio, and Jorge Pérez-López (Summer 1997): "Refugee Remittances, Conceptual Issues, and the Cuban and Nicaraguan Experiences," Center for Migration Studies, *International Migration Review* 31(118):411–37.

Díaz-Briquets, Sergio, and Sidney Weintraub, eds. (1991): *Migration, Remittances, and Small Business Development: Mexico and Caribbean Basin Countries*. Boulder: Westview Press.

Dutta, M. (1982): "Asian Indian Americans: Search for an Economic Profile," in *From India to America*, ed. S. Chandrasekhar. CA: Population Review, pp. 76–85.

Eberstadt, Nicholas (May 1996): "Financial Transfers from Japan to North Korea: Estimating the Unreported Flows," *Asian Survey* 36(5):523–42.

Expert Group Meeting on Remittances from International Labour Migration (September 25, 1985): *Report of the Expert Group Meeting on Remittances from International Labour Migration*. Bangkok: UN.

Fareedy, Fareed A. (Summer/Winter 1984): "Workers' Remittances: A Determinant of International Migration," *Pakistan Economic and Social Review* 22(1/2):65–88.

Fatchamps, Marcel (1992): "Solidarity Networks in Preindustrial Societies: Rational Peasants with a Moral Economy," *Economic Development and Cultural Change* 41(1):147–74.

Funkhouser, Edward (1992): "Mass Emigration, Remittances, and Economic Adjustment: The Case of El Salvador in the 1980s," in George J. Borjas and Richard B. Freeman, eds., *Immigration and the Work Force: Economic Consequences for the United States and Source Areas*. Chicago: University of Chicago Press, pp. 135–77.

García López, José R. (1992): *Las Remesas de los Immigrantes Españoles en América, Siglos XIX y XX*. Oviedo: Ediciones Jucar.

Garson, Jean-Pierre, and Georges Tapinos (1981): *L'Argent des Immigrées: Revenus, Epargne et Transferts de Huit Nationalités Immigrées en France*. Paris: Presses Universitaires de France.

Glytsos, Nicholas P. (October 1993): "Measuring the Income Effects of Migrant Remittances: A Methodological Approach Applied to Greece," *Economic Development and Cultural Change* 42(1):131–68.

Granovetter, M. (1985): "Economic Action and Social Structure: The Problem of Embeddedness," *American Journal of Sociology* 91:481–510.

Hallwood, Paul (Spring 1987): "Labor Migration and Remittances between OPEC Members and Non-Oil LDCs," *Middle East Review* 19(3):39–48.

Helweg, W. H. (1983): "Emigrant Remittances: Their Nature and Impact on a Punjab Village," *New Community* 10(3):435–43.

Hoddinott, John (1994): "A Model for Migration and Remittances Applied to Western Kenya," *Oxford Economic Papers* 46:459–76.

James, K. E. (1991): "Migration and Remittances: A Tongan Village Perspective," *Pacific Viewpoint* 32(1):1–23.

Kaimowitz, David (October 1990): "The "Political" Economies of Central America: Foreign Aid and Labour Remittances," *Development and Change* 21(4):637–55.

Kakar, S. (1998): "Asian Indian Families" in *Minority Families in the United States: A Multicultural Perspective*, ed. R. L. Taylor. NJ: Prentice Hall.

Kalleberg, Arne L., Barbara F. Reskin, and Ken Hudson (2000): "Bad Jobs in America: Standard and Nonstandard Employment Relations and Job Quality in the United States," *American Sociological Review* 65:256–78.

Kandil, M., and M. F. Metwally (June 1990): "The Impact of Migrants' Remittances on the Egyptian Economy," *International Migration* 28(2):159–80.

Katznelson, Ira. (1994): *City Trenches.* Chicago: University of Chicago Press.

Keely, Charles, and Bassam Saket (Autumn 1984): "Jordanian Migrant Workers in the Arab Region: A Case Study of Consequences for Labor Supplying Countries," *Middle East Journal* 38(4):685–98.

Keely, Charles, and Bao Nga Tran (Fall 1989): "Remittances from Labor Migration: Evaluations, Performance, and Implications," *International Migration Review* 23(3).

Khandelwal, M. S. (1995): "Indian Immigrants in Queens, New York City: Patterns of Spatial Concentration and Distribution, 1965–1990," in *Nation and Migration: The Politics of Space in the South Asian Diaspora*, ed. Peter van der Veer. Philadelphia: University of Pennsylvania Press, pp. 178–96.

Lebon, Andre (1984): "Les Envois de Fonds des Migrants et leur Utilisation," *International Migration* 22(4):281–333.

Leonard, K. (1997): *The South Asian Americans.* Westport, CT: Greenwood Press.

Leonhard, S. P. J., et al. (1980): "The Indian Immigrant in America: A Demographic Profile." In *The New Ethnics: Asian Indians in the United States*, eds. E. Eames and P. Saran. New York: Praeger, pp. 136–162.

Lessinger, J. (1995): *From the Ganges to the Hudson: Indian Immigrants in New York City.* Massachusetts: Allyn & Bacon.

Lessinger, J. (1992): "Investing or Going Home? A Transnational Strategy among the Indian Immigrants in the United States," *Annals New York Academy of Sciences* 645:53–80.

Lianos, Theodore P. (Spring 1997): "Factors Determining Migrant Remittances: The Case of Greece," Center for Migration Studies, *International Migration Review* 31(117):72–87.

Loomis, T. (1990): "Cook Island Remittances: Volumes, Determinants, and Uses," in *Migration and Development in the South Pacific*, ed. J. Connell. Canberra: Australia National University, pp. 61–81.

Looney, Robert E. (June 1990): "Worker Remittances in the Arab World: Blessing or Burden?" *Jerusalem Journal of International Relations* 12(2):28–48; (March 1990): "Macroeconomic Impacts of Worker Remittances on Arab World Labor Exporting Countries," *International Migration* 28(1):25–45; (December 1989): "Patterns of Remittances and Labor Migration in the Arab World," *International Migration* 27(4):563–80.

Lozano Ascencio, Fernando (1993): *Bringing It Back Home: Remittances to Mexico from Migrant Workers in the United States*. La Jolla, CA: Center for U.S.-Mexican Studies/University of California, San Diego.

Lucas, Daniel. Greengrocery worker. Interviewed by author December 31, 1999.

Lynd, Staughton (1996): *We Are All Readers*. Urbana: University of Illinois Press, pp. 1–26.

Macpherson, Cluny (Spring 1992): "Economic and Political Restructuring and the Sustainability of Migrant Remittances: The Case of Western Samoa," in *Contemporary Pacific* 4(1):109–35.

Massey, Douglas S., (1987): "Understanding Mexican Migration to the United States," *American Journal of Sociology* 92:1372–1403.

Massey, Douglas S. and Emilio A. Parrado (1994): "Migradollars: The Remittances and Savings of Mexican Migrants to the United States," *Population Research and Policy Review* 13:3–30.

Massey, Douglas S., Jorge Durán, William Kandel, and Emilio A. Parrado (May 1996): "International Migration and Development in Mexican Communities," *Demography* 33(2):249–64.

Massey, Douglas S., Jorge Durán, and Emilio A. Parrado (Summer 1996): "Migradollars and Development: A Reconsideration of the Mexican Case," Center for Migration Studies, *International Migration Review* 30(2):423–44.

Mehta, M. (September 1998): "Exploit of the Indian Techie," *Little India*.

Melwani, L. (January 31, 1994): "Dark Side of the Moon," *India Today*.

Mohammad, Shahida Ali (1987): "Overseas Pakistanis: Problem of Remittance and Rehabilitation," *Pakistan Horizon* 40(3):56–61.

Montes, Segundo (1990): *El Salvador 1989: Las Remesas que Envían los Salvadoreños de Estados Unidos: Consequencias Económicas*. San Salvador: Universidad Centroamericana José Simeón Canas.

Morris, A. (1985): "Taxi School: A First Step in Professionalizing Taxi Driving," *Transportation Research Record* 1103:40–48.

Morris, A., and A. Foster. (January 10–14, 1993): "Changing Demographics of the Taxi Workforce: Implications for Taxi Driver Education," paper presented at the Transportation Research Board.

Ness, Immanuel, and Nick Unger (April 2000): "Union Approaches to Immigrant Organizing: A Review of New York City Locals." UCLEA Labor Education Conference, Milwaukee, Wisconsin.

Oberai, A. S., and H. K. Manmohan Singh (January–February 1980): "Migration, Remittances, and Rural Development: Findings of a Case Study in the Indian Punjab," *International Labour Review* 119(2):229–41.

Pais, Shobha (1997): "Asian Indian Families in America" in *Families in Cultural Context: Strengths and Challenges in Diversity*, ed. Mary Kay DeGenova. CA: Mayfield Publishing.

Penny, N. J. H. (September 1986): "Migrant Labour and the South African Gold

Mining Industry: A Study of Remittances," *South African Journal of Economics* 54(3):290–306.

Perez, Maria Claribel Perez. Member of the Workplace Project and Leader of M.I.L.I. Interviewed by author November 2001.

Pertierra, Raúl, ed. (1992): *Remittances and Returnees: The Cultural Economy of Migration in Ilocos.* Quezon City: New Day Publishers.

Plafero, Eduardo. Member of the Workplace Project and Leader of L.O.V.E.L.I. Interviewed by author January 2002.

Portes, A. (1998): "Social Capital: Its Origins and Applications in Modern Sociology," *Annual Review of Sociology* 24(1):1–24.

———. (1995): *The Economic Sociology of Immigration.* New York: Russell Sage Foundation.

Portes, A., and Jozsef Borocz (1989): "Contemporary Immigration: Theoretical Perspectives on Its Determinants and Modes of Incorporation," *International Migration Review* 23(3):606–30.

Portes, A., and J. Sensebrenner (1993): "Embeddedness and Immigration: Notes on the Social Determinants of Economic Action," *American Journal of Sociology* 98(6):1320–50.

Premi, M. K., and M. D. Mathur (1995): "Emigration Dynamics: The Indian Context," *International Migration,* 33(3–4):627–66.

Preston, Samuel (November 1993): "The Contours of Demography: Estimates and Projections," *Demography* 30(4):593–606.

Quibria, M. G. (1986): "Migrant Workers and Remittances: Issues for Asian Developing Countries," *Asian Development Review* 4(1):78–99.

Regional Conference on the Integration of Women into the Economic and Social Development of Latin America and the Caribbean (November 24, 1988): *Remittances, Family Economy, and the Role of Women: The Case of El Salvador.* Santiago de Chile: UN.

Repak, T. (1995): *Waiting on Washington: Central American Workers in the Nation's Capital.* Philadelphia: Temple University Press.

Restaurant Opportunities Center of New York (2005): *Behind the Kitchen Door: Pervasive Inequality in New York's Thriving Industry.* Report can be found on www.rocny.org.

Rivera-Batiz, Francisco (1986): "International Migration, Remittances, and Economic Welfare in the Source Country," *Journal of Economic Studies* 13(3):3–19.

Rodríguez, Orlando et al. (1995): *Nuestra América en Nueva York: The New Immigrant Hispanic Populations in New York City, 1980–1990.* Hispanic Research Center Report Series, Fordham University, in collaboration with the Institute for Puerto Rican Policy.

Rubenstein, Hymie (1983): "Remittances and Rural Underdevelopment in the English-speaking Caribbean," *Human Organization* 42:295–306. (1992): "Migration, Development, and Remittances in Rural Mexico," *International Migration* 30:127–54.

Rumbaut, R. G. (1996): "Ties That Bind: Immigration and Immigrant Families in the United States," in *Immigration and the Family: Research and Policy on U.S. Immigrants,* ed. Alan Booth, Ann C. Crouter, Nancy S. Landale. NJ: Lawrence Erlbaum Associates.

Russell, Margo (1984): "Beyond Remittances: The Redistribution of Cash in Swazi Society," *Journal of Modern African Studies* 22(4):595–615.

Saket, Bassam K. (1981): *Promoting the Productive Use of Remittances.* Beirut: UN (the case of Jordan).

Saran, Parmatma (1985): *The Asian Indian Experience in the United States.* Cambridge: Schenkman.

Saran, P., and E. Eames (1980): *The New Ethnics: Asian Indians in the United States.* New York: Praeger.

Sassen, Saskia (2000): *The Global City: New York, London, Tokyo*, updated ed. Princeton: Princeton University Press.

———. (1999): *Cities: Between Global Actors and Local Conditions.* University of Maryland Press.

———. (1995): "Immigration and Local Labor Markets," in *The Economic Sociology of Immigration*, ed. A. Portes. New York: Russell Sage Foundation, pp. 87–127.

———. (1988): *The Mobility of Labor and Capital.* New York: Cambridge University Press.

Schaller, Bruce (1994): *The New York City Taxicab Fact Book*, 3rd ed. New York: New York Taxi and Limousine Commission.

Schaller, Bruce, and Gorman Gilbert (1994): "Factors of Producion in a Regulated Industry: New York Taxi Drivers and the Price for Better Service." *Transportation Quarterly*, 49(4) Fall 1995, 81–90.

Schaller, Bruce, and Gorman Gilbert (1994): "Villain or Bogeyman? New York's Taxi Medallion System." *Transportation Quarterly*, Winter 1996, 91–103.

Shankman, P. (1976): *Migration and Underdevelopment: The Case of Western Samoa.* Boulder: Westview Press.

Singh, G., and S. Thandi (1999): "The Unidentical Punjub Twins: Some Explanations of Comparative Agricultural Performance Since Partition," in *Region and Partition*, ed. I. Talbob and G. Singh. Karachi: Oxford University Press.

Spiegel, A. D. (1980): "Rural Differentiation and Diffusion of Migrant Labor Remittances in Lesotho," in P. Mayer, ed., *Black Villagers in an Industrial Society.* Cape Town: Oxford University Press.

Stahl, C., and F. Arnold (1986): "Overseas Workers' Remittances in Asian Development," *International Migration Review* 20:899–925.

Stahl, Charles W., and Ahsanul Habib (September 1989): "The Impact of Overseas Workers' Remittances on Indigenous Industries: Evidence from Bangladesh," in *Developing Economies* 27(3):269–85.

Stanton Russell, Sharon (June 1986): "Remittances from International Migration: A Review in Perspective," *World Development* 14(6):677–96; (1992): "Migrant Remittances and Development," *International Migration* 30:267–87.

Stark, Oded (1992): "Migration in Less Developed Countries: Risk, Remittances, and the Family," *Finance and Development* 28(4):39–41.

Stark, Oded, and Robert E. B. Lucas (April 1988): "Migration, Remittances, and the Family," *Economic Development and Cultural Change* 36(3):465–81; (1985): "Motivations to Remit: Evidence from Botswana," *Journal of Political Economy* 93:901–18.

Stark, Oded, J. Edward Taylor, and Shlomo Yitzhaki (1986): "Remittances and Inequality," *Economic Journal* 96:722–40; (1988): "Migration, Remittances, and

Inequality: A Sensitivity Test Using the Extended Gini Index," *Journal of Development Economics* 28:309–22.

Stinner, William F., Klaus de Albuquerque, and Roy S. Bryce-Laporte, eds. (1982): *Return Migration and Remittances: Developing a Caribbean Perspective.* Washington, DC: Research Institute on Immigration and Ethnic Studies, Smithsonian Institution.

Taylor, J. Edward (1992): "Remittances and Inequality Reconsidered: Direct, Indirect, and Intertemporal Effects," *Journal of Policy Modeling* 14:187–208.

Tongamoa, T. (1990): "Internal Migration, Remittances, and Tonga," *Review* 18:12–18.

United Nations (August 1985): *Prospects for Joint Ventures and Other Forms of Economic Cooperation between Middle Eastern Oil Exporting Countries and the Labour Exporting Developing Countries in the ESCAP Region in the Context of Remittances from Labour Migration.* Bangkok: UN (statistical data).

Varma, N. B. (1980): "Indians as New Ethnics: A Theoretical Note," in *The New Ethnics: Asian Indians in the United States*, ed. P. Saran and E. Eames. New York: Praeger.

Vedachalam, A. (September 1998): "The Blood Suckers," *Little India.*

Vidich, C. (1976): *The New York Cab Driver and His Fare.* Massachusetts: Schenkman.

Wahba, S. (December 1991): "What Determines Workers' Remittances?" *Finance and Development*, 41–44.

Waldinger, R. (1997): "Black/Immigrant Competition Re-Assessed: New Evidence from Los Angeles," *Sociological Perspectives* 40(3):365–86.

———. (1996): *Still the Promised City: African-Americans and New Immigrants in Postindustrial New York.* Cambridge: Harvard University Press.

———. (1995): "The 'Other Side' of Embeddedness: A Case Study of the Interplay between Economy and Ethnicity," *Ethnic and Racial Studies* 18:555–80.

———. (Spring 1994): "The Making of an Immigrant Niche," *International Migration Review* 28:3–30.

———. (March 1992): "Taking Care of the Guests: The Impact of Immigrants on Services, an Industry Case Study," *International Journal of Urban and Regional Research* 16(1)97–113.

———. (1989): "Immigration and Urban Change," *Annual Review of Sociology* 15:211–32.

———. (1986): *Through the Eye of the Needle: Immigrants and Enterprise in New York's Garment Trades.* New York: New York University Press.

Wilawan, K. (1995): "The Immigration of Asian Professionals to the United States: 1988–1990," *International Migration Review* 29(1):7–32.

Wood, Charles H., and Terry L. McCoy (1985): "Migration, Remittances, and Development: A Study of Caribbean Cane Cutters in Florida," *International Migration Review* 19:251–77.

# About the Editors and Contributors

**Monika Batra** was involved with Workers' Awaaz as a core member/organizer from its inception in 1997 until May 2003. Monika received a law degree from the University of California at Berkeley School of Law (Boalt Hall) in May 2001. Monika currently practices immigration law in New York City, where she continues to develop as a worker and a new mother, and continues her commitment to the worker struggle.

**Saru Jayaraman** is a graduate of Yale Law School and the Harvard Kennedy School of Government. In 1992 she founded Women and Youth Supporting Each Other (WYSE), a national nonprofit organization dedicated to supporting young women of color. As attorney/organizer at the Workplace Project, a Latino immigrant worker organizing center, she created the Alliance for Justice, a law and organizing program. Most recently, together with workers from Windows on the World, the restaurant at the top of the World Trade Center, she founded the Restaurant Opportunities Center of New York (ROC-NY), an immigrant workers' center focused on organizing immigrant restaurant workers all over New York City. Among other things, ROC-NY has organized workers to win workplace justice campaigns and launch their own cooperatively owned restaurant. She teaches political science, labor economics, and immigrants' rights at Brooklyn College, Queens College, and New York University.

**Alex Julca** was born in Huanuco, Peru, an Andean town two thousand feet above sea level. He came to New York City in 1989, where, after some time working in construction, he continued his graduate studies in economics at the New School, where he earned a PhD in 1997 with a dissertation on Peruvians' migration to New York City. Currently he works at the United Nations headquarters as economic affairs officer.

**Diditi Mitra** is a Professor of Sociology at Brookdale Community College. Dr. Mitra's recent scholarly work focuses on race, class, and immigration among Punjabi emigrants.

**Immanuel Ness** is Associate Professor in the Political Science Department and Associate Director of the Brooklyn College Graduate Center for Worker Education. Ness is a union and community organizer. His recent work includes *Immigrant Unions and the New U.S. Labor Market* (Temple University Press, 2005). He is editor of *Encyclopedia of American Social Movements* (Sharpe, 2004). He is coauthor of *Book of World Cities* (Macmillan Free Press, 1986) and author of *Trade Unions and the Betrayal of the Unemployed*, published by Routledge in 1998. He is also a contributor of many articles and chapters covering labor and politics, low-wage work, immigrant labor, and labor organizing. Ness coedited *Central Labor Councils and the Revival of the American Unionism* (M.E. Sharpe, 2001). His articles have appeared in *New Political Science*, *Labor Studies Journal*, and *National Civic Review*. His work has also appeared in popular magazines, including The *Nation, Z Magazine, Covert Action Quarterly*, and *In These Times*. Ness is author and editor of five encyclopedias, including the *Encyclopedia of Third Parties in America* (2001). Ness is currently completing a book on outsourcing, offshoring, and immigration.

**Ai-jen Poo** is Special Projects Director at CAAAV: Organizing Asian Communities, and is an organizer with NYC Domestic Workers United.

**Eric Tang** is Program Director of the Youth Leadership Project of CAAAV: Organizing Asian Communities.

# Index